Life Changing Journey

Inspirational Quotes

SERIES V

"Unveiling Wisdom: Inspiring Quotes to Spark Your Life. A Treasury of Inspiration for Cultivating Positivity on Life, Love, Nature, and More."

SHREE SHAMBAV

Life Changing Journey
Inspirational Quotes - Series V
Shree Shambav

Published by Shree Shambav, Tamil Nadu, India
Shree Shambav Ink & Imagination "Where Words Breathe and Imagination Soars"

First Edition, 2025

978-93-342-5187-6

Email:shreeshambav@gmail.com

Web:www.shambav.org

DEDICATION

"Isavasyam idam sarvam yat kim ca jagatyam jagat, tena tyaktena bhunjitha, ma gridhah kasyasvid dhanam"

To the Almighty,

the Divine Masters,

the family who listens,

and my parents who see –

your presence shapes the pages of my life's journey.

"Isavasyam idam sarvam yat kim ca jagatyam jagat"

Meaning: "God encompasses everything you perceive, see, or touch with your sense organs."

DISCLAIMER

This book, *"Life-Changing Journey - Inspirational Quotes: Series V,"* is a heartfelt compilation of personal reflections and insights, born from the author's journey of understanding life and the natural world. Each inspirational quote is a subjective truth—a distillation of experience and thought—meant to serve as a mirror for readers to explore their own perspectives and uncover meaning through the lens of their unique experiences.

The intention behind this book is to share a message imbued with compassion, love, and care. It is designed to inspire readers on their personal journeys and guide them toward discovering the deeper realities of life. This is not a prescriptive manual, but an invitation to pause, reflect, and engage with life's profound yet simple truths.

It's important to acknowledge that neither the content nor the sequence of the quotes is intended to cause harm, discomfort, or conflict with the reader's personal beliefs. Should any part of the book feel unsettling or contradictory to one's convictions, it is purely coincidental and never intentional.

The journey through these quotes is one of openness and fluidity, free from rigid interpretations or dogmatic assertions. The content reflects the author's personal perspective, humbly offered as a source of inspiration and gentle guidance. Readers are invited to engage with the material at their own pace, to reflect deeply, and to adapt the wisdom within to align with their inner truths and life experiences.

Above all, this book aspires to spark joy, nurture connection, and encourage purposeful living. It gently beckons readers to cultivate a life rooted in compassion, integrity, and intentionality, while embracing the beauty of each moment with grace and mindfulness. May the words within these pages illuminate your path as you embark on a transformative journey of self-discovery, growth, and renewal. The journey is uniquely yours, and it is an honour for the author to accompany you, even if only in spirit, as you navigate the unfolding of your life.

With this understanding, readers are encouraged to approach the book with an open mind and heart, recognising that its wisdom is offered not as universal truth but as a collection of insights shaped by the author's personal experiences. You are invited to absorb what resonates, reinterpret what feels unfamiliar, and find your own meaning within these words.

Ultimately, the author's deepest wish is that these reflections serve as a beacon of hope, a source of motivation, and a catalyst for positivity as you embark on your life-changing journey. May this book inspire you to walk your path with courage, grace, and an unwavering belief in the beauty of life's unfolding.

Note - If any part of the book, in any sequence, hurts the reader's sentiments, it would be just out of a sheer accident not intentional

Divine

"In the tender embrace of surrender lies a profound revelation—the raw, unspoken beauty of union. Each ripple of the river becomes a whispered confession, a declaration of belonging to something greater than itself. As the river flows ceaselessly, unveiling its eternal unity with the boundless ocean, so too does the soul, in its sacred act of surrender, unveil its timeless connection to the Divine.

This surrender is not a loss but a metamorphosis of unparalleled grace, where the fragmented self dissolves into the infinite. And in that dissolution, the soul discovers the ineffable depth of its true essence—a profound oneness with the Divine, unbroken and eternal. It is a sacred symphony, an eternal melody that reverberates through the very fabric of existence, calling us back to the home we never truly left."

– Shree Shambav

EPIGRAM

"In the vast silence of existence, where moments stretch into eternity, true wisdom is not found in the noise of achievement, but in the quiet of self-reflection. It is here, in the gentle space between thoughts, that we discover our deepest truths. The path to understanding is not a race to the end, but a journey to the heart."

– Shree Shambav

Life Changing Journey

Inspirational Quotes

Shree Shambav

Shree Shambav is a 23x best-selling author renowned for his transformative works in personal development and spiritual growth.

Dear Cherished Readers

Dear Cherished Readers,

As I embark on this new literary voyage, my heart swells with profound gratitude and an overwhelming sense of connection. With deep emotion, I extend my heartfelt appreciation to each of you who has joined me on this journey.

With sincere warmth, I invite you to revisit the steps we have taken together through the pages of my earlier works. Our odyssey began with "Journey of Soul - Karma," a book that marked my first foray into the world of words and a testament to the raw passion that ignited my writing adventure.

The subsequent chapters of our shared narrative unfolded through the enchanting tapestry of the "Twenty + One" series. Each page turned was a brushstroke on the canvas of our imaginations, painting vivid stories that I hoped would resonate deeply within your hearts.

And how can I forget the transformative journey we embarked on with "Life Changing Journey - 365

Inspirational Quotes Series." Day by day, quote by quote, we delved into reflections that uplifted, inspired, and sought to bring a glimpse of light to our souls.

The release of "Death - Light of Life and the Shadow of Death" promises to shed new light on the timeless mystery of death. Similarly, "Unleashing the Incredible Potential of Programming with Python - Optimum - PYTHON: Ultimate Guide for Beginners Series I" is poised to empower readers with newfound knowledge.

In addition, my technical book, OPTIMUM Python Series II - Exploring Data Structures and Algorithms, delves into advanced concepts in Python programming, offering a comprehensive guide for those seeking to deepen their understanding.

Shree Shambav expands his artistic repertoire with "*Whispers of Eternity: A Symphony of Soulful Verses,*" a heartfelt exploration of the human experience. Alongside this, his "*Whispers of the Soul: A Journey Through Haiku*" distils profound insights into poignant verses. Together, these works showcase his versatility and mastery of soulful expression, inviting readers on a journey of self-discovery. Through his poetry, he weaves a rich tapestry of emotion that resonates deeply with the heart.

Shree Shambav's latest works—*Learn to Love Yourself: A Journey of Discovering Inner Beauty and Strength Through 10 Transformative Rules, The Power of Letting Go: Embrace Freedom and Happiness, A Journey of Lasting Peace—are true treasures of self-discovery, The Entitlement Trap: Get Over It, Get On, Whispers of a Dying Soul: Unspoken Regrets and Unlived Dreams , Whispers of Silence - Unlocking Inner Power through Stillness, The Power of Words - Transforming Speech, Transforming Lives, The Art of Intentional Living - Minimalism for a Life of Purpose and Awakening the Infinite: The Power of Consciousness in Transforming Life.* Each book offers profound insights into personal growth and well-being, guiding readers on a transformative journey toward inner peace and fulfilment.

In addition to these works, Shree Shambav has recently ventured into astrology with the release of Astrology Unveiled – Foundations of Ancient Wisdom Series I to VI, expanding into the realm of metaphysics. These books explore the foundational principles of Vedic astrology, offering readers a rich and practical understanding of this ancient wisdom.

Your unwavering support, enthusiasm to immerse yourself in my writings, and readiness to embark on these journeys with me have been my greatest sources of inspiration. Your input has been a beacon guiding me through the creation process, moulding these stories into containers of passion, emotion, knowledge, and resonance.

As I unveil this new narrative before you, know that your presence, insights, and shared moments have been my companions. The path we have walked together is etched in the annals of my creative evolution, and it's an honour beyond words to have you by my side once more.

Here's to the readers who have illuminated my path with their presence, who have embraced my stories with open hearts, and who have woven themselves into the very fabric of my literary world. Our journey has been a symbiotic dance of writer and reader, a harmony of souls brought together by the magic of storytelling.

With a heart brimming with appreciation and eyes glistening with anticipation, I extend my deepest gratitude for your unwavering support. Thank you for the memories, the shared emotions, and the countless hours spent in the worlds we've crafted together. As we step into this new adventure, let's continue to explore, feel, and discover the boundless horizons that words can unveil.

Warmly,

Shree Shambav

Suggested Reads

FROM BEST-SELLING AUTHOR

Endorsements

"Life Changing Journey - Inspirational Quotes Series" by Shree Shambav is a profound and transformative collection of wisdom that speaks directly to the heart. Each page is filled with insights that transcend the ordinary, guiding readers through the complexities of life with grace, strength, and deep reflection. This book is more than just a collection of quotes—it is a companion for those seeking inspiration, courage, and peace in the midst of life's challenges. The themes explored in this series—self-discovery, embracing change, resilience, and the beauty of simplicity—offer a timeless roadmap for personal growth and inner fulfilment. Shree Shambav's words are a beacon of light, inviting you to embark on a journey of transformation and self-realisation. This is a must-read for anyone looking to reconnect with their true essence and embrace life's profound possibilities.

Nandini (Educationalist)

About the Author

Shree Shambav is a remarkable individual who excels as an author, speaker, philanthropist, life coach, and entrepreneur. With grace and distinction, he has inspired countless individuals through his counselling, teachings, and books, guiding them toward personal transformation.

Shree Shambav is a 23x best-selling author celebrated for his profound contributions to personal development and spiritual growth.

Shree Shambav's literary journey took flight with the celebrated Journey of Soul - Karma, where he delved into the depths of human experience to unveil profound insights. Garnering recognition through multiple literature awards, his repertoire includes esteemed works, such as the Twenty + One Series and the enlightening Life Changing Journey series.

As a distinguished alumnus of the Indian Institute of Management and the National Institute of Technology, Shree Shambav brings a wealth of corporate acumen from his tenure in multinational corporations. His most recent publications, including Unveiling the Enigma, Death - Light of Life and the Shadow of Death and Optimum - Python Series I and Series II, demonstrate his mastery of both the literary and technical spheres.

Shree Shambav expands his artistic repertoire with "*Whispers of Eternity: A Symphony of Soulful Verses*," a heartfelt exploration of the human experience. Alongside this, his "*Whispers of the Soul: A Journey Through Haiku*" distils profound insights into poignant verses. Together, these works showcase his versatility and mastery of soulful expression, inviting readers on a journey of self-discovery. Through his poetry, he weaves a rich tapestry of emotion that resonates deeply with the heart.

Shree Shambav's latest works—*Learn to Love Yourself: A Journey of Discovering Inner Beauty and Strength Through 10 Transformative Rules, The Power of Letting Go: Embrace Freedom and Happiness, A Journey of Lasting Peace—are true treasures of self-discovery, The Entitlement Trap: Get Over It, Get On, Whispers of a Dying Soul: Unspoken Regrets and Unlived Dreams , Whispers of Silence - Unlocking Inner Power through Stillness, The Power of Words - Transforming Speech, Transforming Lives, The Art of Intentional Living - Minimalism for a Life of Purpose and Awakening the Infinite: The Power of Consciousness in Transforming Life.* Each book offers profound insights into personal growth and well-being, guiding readers on a transformative journey toward inner peace and fulfilment.

In addition to these works, Shree Shambav has recently ventured into astrology with the release of Astrology Unveiled – Foundations of Ancient Wisdom Series I to VI, expanding into the realm of metaphysics. These books explore the foundational principles of Vedic astrology, offering readers a rich and practical understanding of this ancient wisdom.

Shree Shambav established the Ayur Rakshita Foundation, which is dedicated to promoting boundless growth, universal fraternity, and environmental protection. The charity helps diverse communities while working for societal progress.

To learn more about Shree Shambav and his works, visit his website at www.shambav.org. For information about the Ayur Rakshita Foundation and its initiatives, visit www.shambav-ayurrakshita.org.

Let's Follow him on Social Media: **@shreeshambav**

PREFACE

Life is a symphony, where each moment plays a unique note in the grand composition of existence. Within this melody, words possess a timeless power—they awaken, heal, and inspire. *"Life Changing Journey - Inspirational Quotes Series"* by Shree Shambav is not just a collection of phrases; it is a companion, a guide, and a beacon for those navigating the intricate pathways of life.

This book was conceived in the quiet spaces where inspiration is born—in those still moments when the noise of the world fades and the soul begins to speak. Every quote in this collection distils universal truths into simple yet profound expressions, echoing the essence of human experience. Through these pages, you are invited to embark on a journey of self-discovery, reflection, and transformation.

The chapters are thoughtfully crafted, each offering a thematic exploration of the human spirit. They illuminate the courage required to embrace change, the resilience to chase dreams, and the wisdom to find meaning amid life's adversities. They delve into love and relationships, the beauty of self-acceptance, and the quiet strength that lies dormant within. These chapters whisper of joy found in simplicity, gratitude awakened through mindfulness, and the profound connection we share with the natural world and the cosmos.

This book is a tapestry woven with timeless insights that transcend circumstances. It invites you to pause, reflect, and draw inspiration from the wellspring of human wisdom. Whether you are weathering life's storms, seeking the motivation to pursue your aspirations, or yearning for the serenity of inner peace, these quotes serve as a trusted guide and confidant.

In Series III, themes like *"Embracing Change," "Discovering Self," "Dreams and Aspirations," "Embracing Imperfections," "Finding Inner Strength,"* and *"Gratitude and Mindfulness"* invite you to reflect on identity, purpose, and the pursuit of your passions.

Series IV delves deeper into *"Inspiration and Motivation," "Lessons from Adversity," "Love and Relationships," "Nature's Symphony," "Pursuing Your Dreams,"* and *"Serenity and Balance"*—nurturing connections, fostering resilience, and celebrating life's harmony.

Series V culminates in the profound, with themes like *"Shades of Existence," "Success and Achievement," "The*

Beauty of Simplicity," "The Power of Kindness," "Whispers of the Divine," and *"Wisdom from the Ages."* These chapters remind us to cherish the beauty in life's simplest moments and draw strength from timeless truths.

Shree Shambav's words transcend the mundane, touching the sacred essence of life. They serve as gentle reminders of our shared humanity, encouraging us to embrace imperfections and live authentically. Each quote is a spark—a catalyst for growth and self-discovery, illuminating the path through life's trials and triumphs.

As you turn these pages, may you find not just words, but a profound connection to your inner self and the world around you. Let this collection be a sanctuary of wisdom, a reservoir of courage, and a wellspring of inspiration, empowering you to embrace life with an open heart and an awakened soul.

Welcome to the *"Life Changing Journey - Inspirational Quotes Series."* May this book inspire you to live boldly, love deeply, and discover the boundless joy within your own journey.

Let the journey unfold.

With gratitude and encouragement,

Shree Shambav

INTRODUCTION

In a world that often feels like a whirlwind of expectations, responsibilities, and endless noise, it's easy to lose sight of the deeper meaning of life. We rush through our days, chasing goals and ticking off to-do lists, yet many of us long for something more—something that grounds us, inspires us, and reconnects us to the beauty of existence.

This longing is the seed from which the *"Life Changing Journey - Inspirational Quotes Series"* was born. At its heart, this book is an invitation—a gentle call to pause, reflect, and rediscover the wisdom that lies within and around us.

Words have an extraordinary ability to shape our perspectives and transform our lives. A single phrase, encountered at the right moment, can shift our understanding, provide clarity in times of confusion, or ignite a spark of courage in the face of fear. This collection of quotes was curated with this transformative power in mind. Each one is a distillation of universal truths, designed to speak directly to the soul and awaken the resilience, hope, and strength that reside within us all.

This book unfolds across a series, each thoughtfully curated to illuminate different dimensions of the human experience. Series I and Series II set the foundation, offering inspiration and insight into the journey of life.

Series V: Embracing the Tapestry of Life

This series is an evocative invitation to delve into the transformative power of change and embark on a deeply personal journey of self-discovery. With themes such as "Shades of Existence," "Success and Achievement," "The Beauty of Simplicity," "The Power of Kindness," "Whispers of the Divine," and "Wisdom from the Ages," these chapters illuminate the profound lessons hidden within life's intricate moments. They remind us to cherish the elegance of simplicity, draw strength from timeless truths, and find purpose amidst the chaos.

Through these heartfelt reflections, you'll uncover the quiet fortitude needed to navigate life's inevitable transitions, the courage to live in alignment with your authentic self, and the boundless joy that arises from embracing gratitude and presence. Each theme is a stepping stone—a bridge to understanding the beauty in imperfection, the growth birthed through adversity, and the enduring strength nestled within your spirit.

This series does more than inspire—it transforms. It offers a guiding light, and a compass to help you find balance, resilience, and purpose in an ever-changing world. As you journey through these pages, you'll traverse a rich tapestry of insights that mirror the multifaceted nature of life. From the bold courage required to face change to the wisdom unearthed through trials, the tenderness of nurturing love and relationships, and the serenity found in simplicity and gratitude—each chapter is a portal to deeper reflection and profound understanding.

This series isn't merely a collection of themes; it's an exploration of life itself—raw, beautiful, and filled with endless possibilities.

This series is not just a collection of words but a companion for your personal growth, offering profound insights that encourage you to live authentically and harmoniously.

But this book is not meant to be read in a rush. It is not a novel to be consumed from cover to cover in one sitting. Instead, it is a companion for life's journey, offering guidance and solace whenever you need it most. You might find comfort in a quote during a moment of despair, draw courage from a phrase when facing a challenge, or uncover a fresh perspective as you navigate a crossroads.

The beauty of this collection lies in its timelessness. Whether you're at the beginning of your journey, in the midst of transformation, or reflecting on lessons learned, these quotes will meet you where you are. They are not answers but mirrors, reflecting the wisdom you already possess and encouraging you to trust your inner voice.

We live in a time where the external world demands so much of us, yet the most profound answers often come from within. This book is a reminder to listen to that quiet voice—the one that whispers truths when the world falls silent. It is a guide to help you realign with your authentic self, find purpose amidst uncertainty, and celebrate the beauty of being alive.

As you turn the pages of this book, my hope is that you discover not just inspiration but a renewed sense of connection—to yourself, to others, and to the world around you. Let these quotes be your compass, pointing you toward a life of greater meaning, joy, and fulfilment.

This journey is yours to take. With each quote, may you find the courage to embrace your unique path and the wisdom to live it fully.

Welcome to the *"Life Changing Journey - Inspirational Quotes Series."* May these words guide you toward the light within and inspire you to create a life that resonates with your truest self.

With love and gratitude,

Warm regards,

Shree Shambav

PROLOGUE

In the stillness of a quiet moment, when the rush of life recedes and the echoes of the world grow faint, a profound truth emerges: life is not measured by the grand milestones we achieve but by the whispers of wisdom we gather along the way. These whispers often come to us disguised as experiences—moments of joy, heartbreak, triumph, and loss—each carrying a lesson, a reminder, or a revelation.

This book is a collection of such whispers. It is not an instruction manual for life nor a doctrine to be followed. Instead, it is a constellation of insights—a gathering of fragments that speak to the heart and soul. Each quote within these pages is a small light, illuminating a path forward, no matter where you find yourself on life's journey.

The inspiration for this book was born not from a single moment but from a series of them—quiet reflections during sleepless nights, fleeting thoughts in the midst of nature's beauty, and the raw emotions felt during life's highs and lows. In these moments, words would surface, offering clarity and comfort, as though the universe itself was speaking through the silence.

Life, after all, is not a straight line but a tapestry woven from the threads of uncertainty and transformation. Each challenge, each triumph, and each quiet moment in between adds a unique hue to our existence. It is through these experiences that we grow, learn, and uncover the essence of who we are.

This book is an invitation to pause amidst the busyness, to reconnect with the wisdom that often gets lost in the noise. It is for the dreamers who long to soar, the seekers searching for meaning, and the wanderers navigating the uncharted territories of their hearts.

As you turn these pages, you will find a mirror reflecting your own journey—your struggles, your hopes, your resilience. These quotes are not bound by time or place; they are universal truths that transcend culture, age, and circumstance. They are reminders of our shared humanity and the limitless potential within us all.

The journey you are about to embark on is one of self-discovery, courage, and hope. It is a journey inward, to the depths of your soul, and outward to the infinite beauty of the world around you. It is a journey of finding not only answers but also the strength to ask the right questions.

May this book serve as your companion, a source of light in moments of darkness and a wellspring of inspiration when you need it most. Let these words guide you, challenge you, and ultimately remind you of the infinite power that lies within your own heart.

Welcome to the *'Life Changing Journey - Inspirational Quotes Series."* This is not merely a book—it is a gift to your soul, a doorway to transformation, and a reminder that every moment holds the potential for greatness.

With hope and love,

Shree Shambav

CONTENTS

DEDICATION iii
DISCLAIMER v
Divine ix
EPIGRAM xi
Dear Cherished Readers xv
Suggested Reads xix
Endorsements xxi
About the Author xxiii
PREFACE xxvii
INTRODUCTION xxxi
PROLOGUE xxxvii
CONTENTS xli
Shades of Existence 1
    Light of life 1
Success and Achievement 39
    Unleashing Your Potential 39
The Beauty of Simplicity 63
    Embracing Life's Little Pleasures 63
The Power of Kindness 91

Spreading Compassion and Love 91
Whispers of the Divine 119
Cosmic connection 119
Wisdom from the Ages 157
Timeless Insights for Life 157
Life Coach and Philanthropist 185
TESTIMONIALS 189
ACKNOWLEDGEMENTS 197
BOOKS BY – AUTHOR 199

Shades of Existence

Light of life

"The light of life shines brightest not in the absence of shadows, but in the way we embrace them. Each shade reveals a hidden truth, and in the interplay of light and dark, we find the full spectrum of our existence."

- *Shree Shambav*

A Guiding Light of Energy

"As I nurture my energy, it becomes a guiding light, illuminating my path and enveloping me in strength and serenity."

A Passage to Transcendence

"The wisdom of the ages teaches us that death is not a termination but a transcendence, a graceful passage into the ultimate truth of our being."

Acceptance and Connection

"In accepting others as they are, we unlock the door to genuine connection and mutual understanding."

Alchemy of Existence

"In the alchemy of existence, only love and death wield the power to transmute all things. Love breathes life into the mundane, while death, the silent maestro, orchestrates the grand finale of transformation."

Alchemy of Spirituality

"Beyond the veil of stillness lies a profound truth: spirituality is the inner alchemy, the sacred science of the soul. It is not a detachment from the physical realm, but a meticulous exploration of the metaphysical. Since time immemorial, the intricate dance between science and spirituality has been woven into the fabric of existence, beckoning us to embark on a journey of self-discovery, where the inner realms unfold as a canvas for the artistry of expanded consciousness."

Anchors of Ascent

"In our quest for self-elevation, our vices and weaknesses act as heavy anchors, ready to pull us down into the depths of despair."

Awakening from Hypnosis

"Living in hypnosis is akin to drifting through a half-life, oblivious to the profound richness that awaits beyond the surface of our daily experiences."

Beacons of Potential

"When the horizon seems shrouded in impossibility, remember that the Guru's blessings and the supreme's grace are the steadfast beacons illuminating the path of potential. With their divine touch, what once appeared beyond reach becomes the realm of the achievable, and the unimaginable transforms into the tapestry of reality."

Canvas of Life

"Life's canvas is painted with both light and shadows, each adding depth and meaning to the masterpiece."

Confidence in the Twilight of Life

Confidence is the unwavering belief that even in the twilight of life, when all seems lost, you have the power to weave your world anew from the threads of resilience."

Courage to Embrace the Unknown

"It takes great courage to release the familiar and embrace the unknown. But in doing so, we open ourselves up to infinite possibilities and invite miracles into our lives."

Courageous Journey of Awakening

"To embark on the journey of awakening is to courageously confront suffering and embrace its transformative potential with an open heart."

Dance of Light and Shadows

"In the tapestry of life, light and shadows dance together, weaving a story of contrast and beauty."

Death as a Sacred Transition

"In the awakening of consciousness, death transforms from an ending into a transition—a sacred doorway to new beginnings."

Death's Peaceful Acceptance

"Death should be a peaceful entry into the unknown, a joyful farewell to the familiar."

Defying the Whispering Darkness

"In the shadows where fear lurks, beckoning with whispered doubts, there lies darkness so profound, it tempts the bravest to falter. 'There, in the wilderness,' it whispers, 'lies danger.' Yet, heed not its call, for true courage resides in the defiance of such whispers, in the unwavering resolve to step into the unknown and emerge, unbroken, into the light."

Discovering Raw Beauty

"In the quiet spaces of unbecoming, where we shed the masks and shed the layers, we discover the raw beauty of our authentic selves."

Divine Perfection

"Perfection comes from the Perfect One."

Echoes Beyond Words

"In the whispers of the wind and the dance of the stars, lies a symphony of ethereal echoes, resonating with the depths of our souls, speaking volumes beyond the confines of mere words."

Echoes of Light

"In the quiet emptiness of our home, your laughter and cries echo as poignant reminders of the light you brought into our lives."

Embracing Diversity

"In the tapestry of humanity, diversity is the vibrant thread that weaves the fabric of our existence. Embrace each individual as a masterpiece of their own creation, for to accept them fully is to honour the richness of their journey. With patience, kindness, and unwavering tolerance, nurture the blossoming souls around you, for it is in this tender embrace that the true beauty of humanity flourishes."

Embracing Suffering as a Teacher

"Embrace suffering as a wise teacher, for within its lessons lie the transformative seeds of profound joy and liberation."

Embracing the Flow of Life

"The liberating practice of letting go teaches us that life is a continuous flow, not a stagnant pond. By embracing the ebb and flow, we align ourselves with the natural rhythm of existence, finding peace in the impermanence of all things."

Enduring Light of Hope

"Life's labyrinthine twists unveil our inner fortitude, illuminating the way forward with the enduring light of hope."

Essence of Spirituality

"Beyond the rituals of religion, the stillness of meditation, and the physicality of yoga lies the essence of spirituality—a sacred journey of the heart and mind, where the soul finds solace in the interconnectedness of all existence."

Eternal Embrace

"In the tender union of river and ocean lies the profound revelation: separation was but an illusion, for they were always one. Similarly, in the sacred surrender to the higher self, a soulful metamorphosis transpires, unveiling the eternal bond with the Divine—an embrace spanning the depths of eternity, where every heartbeat echoes the symphony of unity."

Eternal Gratitude

"Our dearest angel, born with gratitude and cherished with every heartbeat, left us too soon, leaving behind a tapestry of moments etched in our souls."

Every Breath a Prayer

"When life is lived in its fullest, every breath becomes a prayer, every moment a meditation, preparing the soul for the serene embrace of death."

Exploring Life's Narrative

"Our lives are like books. Many judge by the cover, some skim the prologue, and others delve into the introduction. But only a few immerse themselves in the full story, understanding its depth and richness."

Exploring the Soul

"Not all who wander are lost; some are simply exploring the boundless landscapes of their souls, seeking the truths hidden within."

Final Tribute

"Cremation is the final tribute we offer to those who walked this earth, honouring their existence and the indelible mark they left behind."

Finding Light in the Shadows

"Beneath the cloak of deception, where shadows cast doubt upon the path ahead, fear takes root, urging retreat. 'There, in the wilderness,' it warns, 'lies peril.' Yet, do not succumb to its treacherous whispers, for within the depths of uncertainty, lies the essence of discovery. It is in the defiance of fear, in the unwavering trust in one's inner compass, that true enlightenment is found."

Forged in Adversity

"In the depths of adversity lies the crucible of human resilience, where the flames of challenge forge the steel of our spirit, illuminating the path to profound transformation and unwavering strength."

Freedom Beyond Attachments

"In the quiet surrender of letting go, we discover the profound freedom that lies beyond our attachments. It's in releasing our grip on what no longer serves us that we find the true essence of our being."

Guiding Light in the Shadows

"When virtues flourish, the soul becomes a beacon of light amidst the shadows of existence, casting its luminous gaze upon the tangled web of human experience, guiding the incarnated self with a steady hand and an unwavering resolve, forging a union between the divine and the mortal that transcends the boundaries of time and space."

Guiding Souls Through Time

"Amidst the cacophony of voices, it's not the loudest that resonate, but the soft whispers of wisdom that echo through the corridors of time, guiding souls towards enlightenment."

Harmony of Souls

"Amidst the symphony of life, every soul carries its own melody, its own rhythm. Embrace the discordant notes and the harmonious tunes alike, for each contributes to the grand composition of existence. With patience as your guide, kindness as your melody, and tolerance as your harmony, cultivate the young souls around you, nurturing their potential and honouring their individuality."

Harmony of the Seasons

"In the serenade of seasons, nature conducts a symphony of life, each note echoing the eternal dance of birth, growth, decay, and rebirth. Through poetry in nature's rhythm, we find solace in the ever-changing melody of existence, reminding us of the profound interconnectedness of all things."

Honouring Sacredness

"To live sensitively is to honour the sacredness of all life, recognising that each moment holds the potential for deep spiritual growth."

Humour's Light

"A sense of humour is the light that brightens our darkest days, allowing us to savour life's moments and face its challenges with grace and resilience."

Illuminated Path

"In the journey of spiritual development, clarity of vision illuminates the path, guiding us towards truth, and empowering us to take meaningful actions."

Illuminating the Soul's Journey

"In the mastery of virtues, the soul ascends to a realm where the echoes of its essence resonate with profound clarity, weaving an intricate tapestry of connection between the ethereal and the earthly, granting the spirit dominion over the flesh."

Immersed in the Ocean of Consciousness

Those who dwell in awareness find themselves immersed in the boundless ocean of consciousness, where the ebb and flow of suffering and joy are but the natural rhythms of existence."

The intertwining of Suffering and Joy

"In the depths of awareness, suffering and joy intertwine, weaving the tapestry of existence with threads of wisdom and compassion."

Jesus' Journey

"In the sacred narrative of Jesus' earthly pilgrimage, each chapter resonates with the profound chords of divinity—from Bethlehem's simplicity to the resurrection's triumphant crescendo, a symphony of eternal echoes."

Jesus' Odyssey

"Jesus' Odyssey is woven with threads of humility, love, and redemption. His journey is an emotional sonnet, echoing the depths of divine love and the promise of eternal hope from the dusty lanes of Nazareth to the sacred sermon on Galilee's mount."

Liberation in Suffering's Seed

"True liberation is found in recognising that within every moment of suffering lies the seed of profound growth and enlightenment."

Luminous Odyssey

"Siddhartha's odyssey echoes through the ages, a luminous journey from palace splendours to the enlightenment of the Bodhi tree. His teachings, like a guiding light, illuminate the path from suffering to liberation, echoing all things' impermanence."

Mired in Mud

"Like deep, clinging mud, our vices and weaknesses bind us to the earth, impeding our upward journey toward enlightenment. Without purification, these muddy depths harden around us, rendering our efforts to rise futile. Only through the transformative power of self-reflection and purification can we soften the mire and emerge victorious in our quest for elevation."

Navigating Life's Journey with Ancestral Guidance

"Like the gentle tide that washes upon the shore, the love and wisdom of those who came before us envelop us in a comforting embrace, guiding us through the vast expanse of existence. In their words and actions, we find echoes of our own longing for meaning and purpose, reminding us that we are never truly alone on this journey called life."

Navigating Life's Tempests

"Amidst the chaos of life's tempests, the seeds of hope take root, blossoming into beacons of light that guide us through the darkest nights, reminding us that even in the depths of despair, the human spirit endures."

Opening Up to Possibilities

"Letting go is not about giving up, but about opening up to the boundless possibilities that await us. It's in the act of release that we make space for growth, healing, and the beauty of the unknown."

Power of Intention

"Each thought, each word, carries the weight of our intentions, shaping not only our own reality but also the paths of those we touch. In the delicate dance of existence, even the faintest whispers of negativity can cast shadows upon the hearts of others, hindering their growth and dimming the light within. Let us tread gently, mindful of the power we wield in thought and speech, for in nurturing kindness and compassion, we pave the way for collective evolution and radiant transformation."

Pure Wonder

"Children, in their purest form, approach life with wonder and acceptance, unburdened by the fears and anxieties imposed by society."

Purpose of Suffering in Awakening

Awakening is not about avoiding suffering, but about illuminating its profound purpose on the path to self-realisation and inner peace."

Quiet Acts of Wisdom

"The monk's brief time with us taught that true wisdom lies not in grand gestures, but in the quiet acts of kindness and foresight that build a stronger community."

Radiance of True Transformation

"True transformation isn't just about growth; it's about courageously peeling away the falsehoods until only the truth of our soul remains, unobscured and radiant."

Reclaiming Your Essence

"In the final stages of life, confidence shines as the faith that you can reclaim and reconstruct your essence, no matter how many times it has been broken."

Rediscovering Innocence

"Embracing the evenness of the mind requires detachment from societal conditioning and a deep rediscovery of our inner selves, much like reclaiming the lost innocence of childhood."

Reflections of Wisdom

"In the reflection of life's mirror, desire gathers as dust, clouding the clarity of one's wisdom. Yet, with the tender touch of self-awareness, the dust settles, unveiling the pristine depth of knowledge that lies beneath."

Resilience and Redemption in Prayer

"Amidst the symphony of longing hearts, woven into the fabric of the universe, we uncover the profound beauty of resilience and the transformative power of faith."

Sacred Act of Respect

"In the sacred act of cremation, we pay our deepest respects, acknowledging the lives that once intertwined with ours and the contributions they made to the world."

Sculpting Humanity

"As the sculptor shapes the marble with a delicate touch, so does the softness of heart and tongue carve the masterpiece of humanity, infusing the world with the sublime flavours of empathy, compassion, and kindness."

Seeds of Stewardship

"As we stand at the crossroads of environmental crisis, let us heed the clarion call to action and sow the seeds of change in the fertile soil of our children's hearts. Through the simple act of nurturing a tree, we imbue them with the profound understanding that our destinies are intertwined with the fate of the natural world, igniting a flame of stewardship that illuminates the path to a brighter tomorrow."

Siddhartha's Saga

"In the sacred pages of Siddhartha's journey, each chapter reveals the profound tapestry of enlightenment— from princely seclusion to the boundless expanse of wisdom, a timeless guide through life's labyrinth."

Silent Depths of Wonder

"In the silent depths of the ocean, the fish glides, unseeing the treasure trove of life around it. So too, we traverse our days, often ignorant of the extraordinary that quietly surrounds us, waiting to be discovered."

Solemn Farewell

"Cremation stands as a solemn farewell, a reverent honour bestowed upon those who shared this earthly journey and enriched it with their presence."

Strength in Acceptance

"True strength lies in embracing others as they are, nurturing bonds that transcend differences."

Tales of Longing and Love

"In the hushed embrace of moonlight, whispers weave tales of longing and love, painting the canvas of night with the hues of emotion."

Tapestry of Hinduism

"Hinduism is not just a religion; it is a dynamic and diverse tradition woven from the threads of indigenous beliefs, philosophical inquiries, and cultural interactions, reflecting the vibrant tapestry of Indian heritage."

The Art of Letting Go

"Letting go does not mean erasing the past or denying its significance. It is about releasing the grip of attachment, surrendering to the flow of existence, and trusting in the wisdom of the universe."

The Beauty of Inner Awakening

"When I embraced the winds of change, I found myself shedding layers of old beliefs and behaviours. This journey inward awakened a profound shift in my perspective, revealing the boundless beauty of impermanence and the infinite potential within each new beginning."

The Blossoming Culmination

"The beauty of death is revealed only to those who have learned to live fully, for it is not an end, but the ultimate, blossoming culmination of life."

The Crescendo of Life

"Death, far from being an enemy, is the crescendo of life—a beautiful, final note that completes the symphony of our existence."

The Delicate Dance of Life

"Each breath is a delicate thread connecting life and death, a poignant dance that underscores the beauty and impermanence of our journey."

The Depth of Life's Moments

"Life's greatest peaks are not in its length but in the depth of each lived moment, where every experience enriches the soul."

The Essence of Peace

"Expecting life to be free of difficulties is a recipe for perpetual disappointment; true peace lies in performing our duties with dedication and relinquishing attachment to the outcomes."

The Essence of True Maturity

"True maturity transcends mere age; it is defined by the depth of awareness and presence one brings to every fleeting moment of existence."

The Grace of Surrender

"True liberation comes when we surrender the need to control the currents of life and instead, float gracefully with the ebb and flow of existence."

The Heart of Creativity

"Creativity transcends competition, offering a profound satisfaction that springs from the heart and nourishes the soul."

The Journey of Self-Transformation

"Self-transformation is not a destination but a journey of awakening, where we shed old beliefs and fears, emerging as the empowered architects of our own destiny."

The Path to Enlightenment

"The path to enlightenment demands embracing both pain and pleasure with equal grace and unwavering awareness."

The Path to Profound Growth

"In the quiet depths of self-discovery, we find the courage to embrace our vulnerabilities, knowing that therein lies the path to profound growth and inner peace."

The Prelude to Death

"A life lived fully in the present prepares the soul for the ultimate flowering that is death, turning it from a feared end into a cherished culmination."

The Quiet Wisdom of the Heart

"In the symphony of life, knowledge may sing its melody, but it's the quiet wisdom of the heart that conducts the true harmony of existence."

The Symphony of Life

"Every experience, every person we meet, every joy and sorrow, contributes to the grand symphony of our lives, with death as the final, perfect note."

The Tapestry of Our Soul's Journey

"In the tapestry of life, every thread, whether bright or dark, weaves the intricate pattern of our soul's journey toward wisdom."

The Timeless Rhythms of Life

"As the seasons serenade us with their poetic dance, we are reminded of the timeless rhythms of nature's song. In the whisper of the wind, the rustle of leaves, and the gentle embrace of sunlight, we find echoes of our own journey, woven into the fabric of the universe's eternal tapestry."

The True Value of Presence

"Only when we lose what we took for granted do we realise its true value. The monk's presence was a blessing; his departure, a profound lesson."

Threads of Legacy

"In the shadow of materialism's grasp, we risk severing the delicate threads that bind us to the natural world, forsaking the wisdom of our ancestors and endangering the legacy we leave for those who follow. Are we not bartering our future for fleeting gains, neglecting the sanctity of the earth beneath our feet?"

Transcending Illusions in Awakening

"To awaken is to transcend the illusions of pain and pleasure, acknowledging both as integral parts of the human journey."

Transforming Fear into Wisdom

"As I surrendered to the transformative waves of personal change, I felt the chains of past fears dissolve. Each moment of acceptance brought a profound shift, turning wounds into wisdom and shadows into light, allowing me to step into the fullness of my true self with grace and purpose."

True wealth

"True wealth lies not in material abundance but in the depths of your understanding. Knowledge is the enduring currency that enriches your journey, immune to the erosion of time."

True Yoga

"The balanced mindset, free from the highs of success and the lows of failure, epitomises true yoga."

Unexpected Paths of Truth

"The pursuit of truth frequently leads down unexpected paths, and the ideal teacher may be discovered in the modesty of an elderly man's dance rather than in grandiosity."

Unveiling Enlightenment

"The search for a perfect master unveils not on majestic peaks but in the echoes of a simple dance, teaching that enlightenment resides in the rhythm of life."

Unveiling Truth

"Amidst the tangled web of uncertainty, where whispers of deceit dance on the wind, tread cautiously, for falsehoods abound. 'Here, in the inner rooms,' they murmur, 'lies truth.' But do not be swayed by their seductive promises, for truth is not found in the shadows of secrecy. It is in the relentless pursuit of clarity, in the unwavering commitment to unveil the light that dispels the darkness."

Veiled Essence

"The essence of the soul is veiled to those who only scratch the surface of life; only those who dare to dive deep can discover the priceless treasure within."

Whispers of Time

"Time passes like wind, weaving stories that flood our senses with memories both cherished and bittersweet."

The Hidden Storms

"Not everyone who boards your ship is a navigator; some are storms in disguise, testing the strength of your vessel and the resilience of your soul."

The Crew of Dreams

"The crew you choose determines the journey you take; trust those who mend your sails, not those who cast anchors in your dreams."

The Helm of Trust

"Every ship needs a steady hand at the helm, but beware the ones who steer with hidden intentions, for they can sink even the most unsinkable vessel."

On Resilience

"The storm tests the strength of the tree, but it is the roots that determine whether it stands or falls."

On the Journey of Life

"Do not chase the horizon; walk steadily, and it will unfold before you."

On Purpose and Passion

"A candle loses nothing by lighting another; instead, the world grows brighter."

On Inner Peace

"Silence is not the absence of noise, but the presence of understanding."

On Embracing Change

"The river does not resist the rocks; it flows around them, shaping them over time. True strength is found not in resistance but in adaptation."

Success and Achievement

Unleashing Your Potential

"Success is not the destination, but the unfolding of your potential in every step you take. Achievement is born from the courage to push past your limits, to rise again after every fall, and to trust in the power of your own growth."

- *Shree Shambav*

Ascending Horizons

"In the quest to empower the mind and spirit, we transcend the constrictions of our own limitations, granting ourselves the freedom to ascend to new horizons on the majestic wings of untapped potential."

Boundless Freedom

"In the limitless blue, a bird knows no boundaries—only freedom. Rise above doubts, and embrace the open sky as your path."

Clarity in the Pause

"It is in the space between breaths, the pause between thoughts, where we find clarity, purpose, and the wisdom to move forward with intention."

Connection as the True Measure

"The real measure of success is not in how high you climb, but in how deeply you connect—with yourself, with others, and with the present moment."

Courage in Persistence

"In the tapestry of life, every thread of effort, no matter how seemingly futile, weaves a story of resilience. Keep trying, for each attempt brings you closer to the moment of triumph."

Courage in Self-Reflection

"In the quiet moments of self-reflection, we find the courage to face our truths; it's in embracing our vulnerabilities that we discover the strength to rise anew."

Courage in the Presence of Hope

"Courage is not the absence of fear, but the presence of hope despite it."

Declaration to Success

"With each step forward, I declare to success, 'I am coming for you,' and I won't retreat until we stand side by side."

Embracing Growth: A Soul's Nourishment

"To nourish your soul is to embrace the discomfort of growth, knowing that each moment of care, each act of alignment, brings you closer to the truest version of yourself."

Faith in the Journey

"A bird trusts the sky beneath its wings, never doubting the next gust. Let your heart be as fearless, gliding through life's unknowns with grace."

Fear's Discernment

"Fear, though commonly regarded as a burden, is the silent guardian of our existence, urging caution and vigilance in the face of danger. However, we must discern between the fears born of tangible threats and those fashioned by the whims of our imagination."

Fearless Flight

"A bird doesn't fear the wind; it lets the breeze carry it to places unseen. Trust the vastness of your journey and soar."

Finding Beauty in Brokenness

"Amidst the wreckage of yesterday, courage whispers its promise: 'Begin again.' For in the rubble lies the raw material of redemption, where shattered fragments pave the path to a mosaic of renewal."

Finding Strength in Adversity

"In the crucible of pain, where suffering beckons, it's our choice where to cast our gaze. For if we dwell on the hurt, we remain shackled to its chains, but if we turn our attention to the lessons learned, we find the strength to grow and thrive."

Flames of Transformation

"Initiating change requires not an army, but a courageous few, who, with hearts ablaze, ignite the flame of transformation that illuminates the path for generations to follow."

Hands of the Bold

"Initiating change is not about the multitude; it's about the audacity of a few, for history attests that the course of humanity has often been altered by the hands of the bold and the determined."

Igniting Transformation

"In the journey of personal development, our growth extends far beyond ourselves; with each step forward, we ignite the potential for transformation in those around us. As we evolve, our influence ripples outward, catalysing progress not just within our own lives, but also within the tapestry of the world we inhabit."

Intentional Self-Care: A Journey of Purpose

"When we care for ourselves with intention, we honour not just our bodies and minds, but the moral compass within, ensuring that each step forward is taken with purpose and truth."

Invitation to Growth

"When we say 'I don't know,' we open ourselves to the world, inviting the power to listen, to question, and to grow beyond our current understanding."

Inviting Fear as a Guide

"When we stop running from our fears and instead invite them in, we discover that they were never meant to paralyse us, but to guide us towards our greatest growth."

Listening to the Soul's Whispers

"Growth begins when we stop seeking validation from others and start listening to the whispers of our soul."

Miraculous Trust

"Miracles are not bestowed upon you; they emerge from the sanctuary of your trust. Like a quiet alchemist, your unwavering faith transmutes the ordinary into the extraordinary, turning the mundane into the magical with each beat of your believing heart."

Nurturing the Roots of Our Soul

"In the quiet moments of stillness, we find that self-nurturing is not about indulgence, but about tending to the roots of our soul, growing stronger in the integrity that defines us."

Relentless Pursuit

"Chasing success is not a journey; it's a relentless pursuit, and I am its unwavering companion."

Resilience in Silence

"A smile amidst life's trials is not a sign of surrender, but a testament to your inner strength, a quiet assurance that even the darkest days cannot break your spirit."

Resilience's Triumph

"Amid the embers of adversity, the phoenix of our resilience ascends, its wings painted with the hues of endurance, transforming the ashes of challenges into the vibrant plumes of triumph."

Rhythm of Progress

"True victory in the pursuit of advancement is found in the commitment to continue doing what is good even when mastery appears to be far away. Each stride, each minute of struggle, brings us closer to the rhythm of progress and harmony."

Ripples of Kindness

"The most profound changes often emerge from the smallest acts of kindness; like ripples on a pond, our gentle gestures can alter the course of someone's life in ways we may never fully comprehend."

Sentinel of Fear

"Fear serves as both a sentinel and a saboteur in the maze of life, guiding our steps in treacherous terrain while ensnaring our minds in the web of illusion. To navigate wisely, we must discern the whispers of genuine danger from the cacophony of imagined threats."

Shine with Authenticity

"When you shine with authenticity, your reflection becomes a beacon of hope, inspiring others to discover their own light."

Solace in Self-Appreciation

"Amidst the shadows of unacknowledged toil, find solace in the light of self-appreciation. Embrace your uniqueness, for in the darkness, your achievements shine brightest."

Sparks of Change

"A single spark of determination can ignite the fields of change. It only takes a handful of visionary hearts to compose the harmonies of a better tomorrow in the symphony of evolution."

Standing Firm in Convictions

"Telling the truth is an act of courage, for it requires us to stand firm in our convictions amidst the world's ever-changing tides."

Stars Born from Darkness

"The darkest nights of the soul often birth the brightest stars within us."

The Bridge of Words

"When words are spoken with clarity and empathy, even the deepest divides can be bridged, for good communication is the quiet force behind every lasting solution."

The Craft of Communication

"Communication is a craft, and like any craft, it flourishes through mindful practice. The more you put into it, the more your voice will reflect the depth of your soul."

The Depths of Success

"Success is not measured by how much you achieve, but by how deeply you live, how fully you love, and how authentically you show up in each moment."

The Fragility of Trust

"Trust is the rarest currency; it takes years to earn but can vanish in a heartbeat, leaving a void that time struggles to fill."

The Intersection of Discomfort and Hope

"True growth begins at the intersection of discomfort and hope; it is the willingness to embrace the unknown that transforms our fears into stepping stones towards our dreams."

The Journey Inward

"In the stillness of your heart lies a profound truth: that the journey inward is far more rewarding than the path that leads outward."

The Key to Conflict Resolution

"At the heart of every conflict lies a conversation yet to be had; good communication is the key that unlocks resolution and understanding."

The Light Within

"We often chase what glitters in the distance, only to realise that the brightest light has always been within us, waiting for us to notice."

The Masterpiece of Character

"The greatest act of self-love is not in seeking ease, but in chiselling away at what no longer serves us, revealing the masterpiece of character that lies beneath."

The Measure of Inner Peace

"True strength is not measured by the battles we win, but by the peace we cultivate within ourselves."

The Mirror of Communication

"The clarity of your communication mirrors the clarity of your mind—nurture it with intention, and your words will resonate with power and purpose."

The Path of Perseverance and Dedication

"Excellence is not a destination but a choice—a commitment to perseverance, dedication, and unwavering resolve. In the absence of shortcuts, we find the true essence of success, illuminated by the sweat and tears of relentless effort."

The Path to Mastery

"Every attempt, whether it ends in success or failure, is a step towards mastery. Each try enriches us with new experiences, slowly crafting our path to the desired outcome."

The Path to Understanding

"Your ability to communicate is determined by the effort you make to understand yourself. The more you develop it, the more your words become a conduit for deeper connection and comprehension."

The Power of a Smile

"If life is a battlefield, let your smile be both armour and weapon—a gentle defiance that radiates strength even in the fiercest of storms."

The Power of Persistence

"Mastery is achieved via persistence rather than perfection. True harmony is achieved not by doing everything right the first time, but by having the courage to keep trying, learning, and improving with each attempt."

The Power of Scars

"Every scar tells a story of resilience, a chapter where pain was transformed into power."

The Power of Truth

"In a world where deception thrives, telling the truth is a revolutionary act of bravery, a testament to our commitment to authenticity and moral clarity."

The Quiet Peace of True Success

"True success is not found in the applause of the world, but in the quiet moments when your heart is at peace with whom you are becoming."

The Silence of True Love

"True love is not measured by the words we say, but by the silence we share when no words are needed."

The Soul's Whispering Strength

"In the whispers of the soul, we find the strength to rise above the noise of the world."

The Symphony of Authentic Living

"To live authentically is to honour the whispers of our soul, for when we align our actions with our values, we create a symphony of purpose that resonates far beyond our existence."

The Tapestry of Life

"In the tapestry of life, every thread—each joy, sorrow, and lesson—adds to our unique design; it is through the interplay of light and shadow that we uncover the beauty of our journey."

The Thread of Compassion

"In the face of life's challenges, clear and compassionate communication is the thread that binds us together, turning problems into opportunities for growth."

The Transformative Power of Reflection

"The strength in your reflection can ignite a transformation in others, revealing the boundless potential within them."

The True Essence of Self-Care

"True self-care is not the art of comfort, but the discipline of aligning with your deepest values, even when the path is steep and uncertain."

The Warrior's Smile

"In the war of life, a true warrior wears a smile—not to mask the pain, but to rise above it, turning every struggle into a symbol of resilience and hope."

The Weight of Belief

"Belief is a simple word with profound weight, for it is more precious than gold and harder to earn than riches."

Threads of Life

"Life is a tapestry made of highs and lows, each thread adding to the beauty of our individual story."

Treasures of the Unexpected

"Life's greatest treasures are often hidden in the places we least expect; sometimes, we must close our eyes to truly see what matters most."

Trust's Alchemy

"No hands, but yours can forge miracles, yet within the crucible of trust, you become the conjurer of wonders. Trust is the silent architect, crafting the unseen bridges that connect you to the extraordinary realms of possibility."

Unravelling Yesterday's Tapestry

"In the tapestry of time, yesterday's threads weave the fabric of today's reality. To truly understand the present, one must unravel the intricate knots of the past, where every thread tells a story of resilience, growth, and profound transformation."

Unseen Resilience

"In the silence of unrecognised efforts lies the resilience of true dedication. When appreciation is scarce, let self-acknowledgment be your loudest applause."

The Beauty of Simplicity

Embracing Life's Little Pleasures

"The beauty of simplicity lies not in the absence of complexity, but in the clarity it brings. When we pause to savour life's small pleasures, we uncover treasures hidden in plain sight, reminding us that true happiness is found in what is simple and pure."

- *Shree Shambav*

Blossoms of Joy

"Within the garden of the present, joy blossoms as a vibrant bloom we delicately pluck, its sweet fragrance a gentle reminder that life's beauty is intricately woven into each fleeting moment."

Celestial Wonder

"In the vast canvas of the night sky, the moon wonders in awe as the stars dance like radiant jewels across the celestial ocean."

Choice of Happiness

"Being happy is a choice. Don't let other people's negativity bring you down; instead, choose to be happy."

Communing with the Divine

"In silence, the soul communes with the divine, transcending the chaos of the world. Across ancient traditions, silence has been a sacred bridge—a space where the veil between the material and the spiritual thins, allowing wisdom and peace to flow from realms beyond words."

Conducting Life's Symphony

"In the symphony of existence, the mind registers the rhythms of facts and frequencies, but it is the gentle touch of the heart that awakens the soul's symphony. With each tender connection, the mind becomes not just an observer but a sensitive conductor, attuned to the harmonies of empathy and compassion."

Courage Beyond Fear

"Courage is found in the moments we choose to face our fears, not because we are unafraid, but because we believe in something greater."

Crafting Happiness

"Born into a world of possibilities, we carry within us the innate skill to craft happiness. It's not a destination; it's the melody we compose, note by note, with the instrument of our existence."

Crafting Life's Tapestry

"In the delicate artistry of life, the quality of our words weaves the fabric of existence, crafting a tapestry of beauty and grace."

Creating Peace Amidst Clamour

"Amidst the relentless clamour of modern life, silence is not found—it is created. By intentionally pausing, turning inward, and embracing stillness, we discover that peace is not the absence of noise, but the presence of mindful awareness in the heart of the chaos."

Cultivating an Inner Sanctuary

"True stillness is not about fleeing the world's cacophony, but rather about cultivating an inner sanctuary where calm and tranquillity can thrive. We learn through mindful practices and moments of detachment that stillness is always accessible, even in the busiest of lives."

Curating Tranquillity

"In the sanctuary of a tidy home, every object serves a purpose and tells a story; as we curate our surroundings, we also curate our inner world, inviting tranquillity into our lives."

Currency of Happiness

"In the symphony of existence, the currency of happiness transcends the confines of monetary value. It resonates in the simple joys of a sunrise, the warmth of a shared embrace, and the melodies of laughter echoing through the corridors of the heart."

Discovering Your True Self

"In the stillness of the mind, the soul finds its voice, and in its whisper, you discover your true self."

Disentangling the True Self

"In the quiet, we find the rare space to disentangle our true selves from the noise of the world. Silence strips away the layers of expectation and fear, revealing the authentic voice within—the one that knows who we are and what we seek."

Echoes of Joy

"Within the realm of soulful action, you harmonise with the gentle whispers of the wind, echoing the joy that resides within, illuminating paths of happiness wherever your footsteps tread."

Embrace Life's Beauty

"Life is too short to waste it in misery. Choose to be happy by looking for the good in every situation."

Embrace the Present

"Living in the moment means letting go of the past and not waiting for the future. It means embracing each breath as a gift, fully conscious of the preciousness of now."

Embracing Change

"Embrace change as the natural rhythm of life, for it is through the ebbs and flows, the highs and lows, that we grow and inspire those who journey with us."

Embracing Your Uniqueness

"Embrace the facets that set you apart, for it is in your uniqueness that the universe reveals its masterpiece."

Emotional Whispers in Stillness

"In the embrace of silence, buried emotions surface like whispers long forgotten, inviting us to face our inner wounds with compassion. It is in this stillness that we allow ourselves the space to heal, finding strength not in avoidance, but in quiet reflection and release."

Equilibrium of Life

"In the delicate dance of life, find your equilibrium - a symphony played between the notes of control and the grace of letting go. True mastery is found in the art of living between effort and surrender."

Freedom Beyond Fear

"Freedom is not found in escaping fear but in embracing it, understanding it, and walking hand in hand with it. True liberation lies beyond fear's illusion."

Freedom's Flight

"In the vast sky of possibilities, let freedom be the kite of your aspirations, its flight guided by the threads of mindful choices, ensuring it soars to great heights without losing touch with the ground."

Harmonising Growth

"The delicate balance of nature teaches us that personal growth, when harmonised with our surroundings, can create ripples of profound and lasting positive change."

Heart's Lullay

"With each whispered refrain, the lullaby sweet of my heart serenades the symphony of emotions, embracing the silence with the gentle cadence of love's eternal song."

Humility and Transformation

"In moments of deep humility and awe, we find the strength to forgive, to understand, and ultimately, to transform our lives and the lives of others for the better."

Inner Radiance

"In the profound journey of understanding, true beauty is discovered not on the skin's surface but in the inner radiance that lights up the soul."

Living in Harmony with Nature

"To live in harmony with nature is to understand its rhythms and cycles as our own. In honouring the earth, we honour the divine life flowing within us."

Love's Garden

"Life reveals its secrets in the peaceful haven of solitude, but love blooms in the garden of togetherness."

Melody of Enlightenment

"The purest melody emerges from the freedom of thought amidst the cacophony of opinions. The soul finds its voice in the vast void of unrestricted contemplation, echoing the core of true comprehension and enlightenment."

Mending the Mind in Silence

"Silence is the haven where the mind learns to mend. It gives us the gift of time—time to go through our emotions, face our suffering, and rebuild our resilience. Silence allows us to recover the confidence to feel deeply, transforming vulnerability into a source of lasting inner calm."

Nature's Symphony

"Miracles, the whispers of nature's hidden symphony, illuminate the boundless potential nestled within the laws of the universe, unveiling the awe-inspiring beauty of cosmic harmony."

On Embracing Vulnerability

"Vulnerability is the gateway to authentic connection, a brave surrender to our innermost truths. In baring our souls, we invite others to do the same, creating a space where genuine love and understanding can flourish."

On Finding Inner Peace

"Inner peace is the quiet haven amidst life's storms, a sanctuary where our soul can rest and rejuvenate. It is found not in the absence of chaos but in the serenity we cultivate within, a gentle reminder of our enduring strength."

On the Beauty of Presence

"Presence is the art of truly being, a mindful engagement with the world around us. In savouring each moment with our full attention, we uncover the profound beauty and depth of our everyday experiences."

On the Essence of Hope

"Hope is the beacon that guides us through the darkest nights, a flicker of light that never wanes. It whispers of possibilities and dreams yet to be realised, reminding us that every dawn brings a new beginning."

On the Essence of True Joy

"True joy is not found in fleeting pleasures but in the deep wellspring of our being. It is the quiet contentment that arises from living in harmony with our values, nurturing our passions, and sharing our light with the world."

On the Journey of Forgiveness

"Forgiveness is the balm that heals the wounds of our spirit, a liberating act of letting go. It frees us from the shackles of resentment, allowing our hearts to breathe and our souls to soar once more."

On the Journey of Healing

"Healing is a sacred journey of reclaiming our wholeness, a tender process of mending the fragments of our soul. With each step, we gather the courage to face our pain and transform it into a tapestry of resilience and grace."

On the Power of Gratitude

"Gratitude is the light that illuminates our journey, revealing the hidden blessings in every moment. In appreciating the small wonders of life, we open our hearts to an abundance of joy and contentment."

On the Power of Resilience

"Resilience is the quiet defiance against life's hardships, a steadfast commitment to rise after every fall. It is in the trials and tribulations that we discover our unbreakable spirit and our boundless capacity for renewal."

On the Strength in Compassion

"Compassion is the bridge that connects hearts, a gentle force that softens the hardest of souls. It is in the act of understanding and sharing another's pain that we find the true strength of our humanity."

Patience and Compassion

"Be patient and compassionate with yourself and others, for true transformation is a tender, slow dance that requires time, understanding, and grace."

Present Awareness

"Living in the moment involves shedding the weight of yesterday and not anticipating tomorrow. It is about consciously appreciating each breath, understanding that every moment is a precious gift."

Self-Acceptance Rain

"The nourishing rain of self-acceptance saturates the soil of our being, allowing the roots of our worth to drink deeply. We bloom with the radiant beauty of our unapologetic truth in this fertile ground."

Self-Compassion as Strength

"To forgive oneself is not an act of weakness but of immense strength. Only when we hold ourselves with compassion, can we begin to free others from judgment as well."

Silence as a Force for Transformation

"In the absence of noise, the brain finds its rhythm, regenerating cells, restoring clarity, and rewiring itself for resilience. Silence, once overlooked, emerges as a potent force for mental and physical health, offering not only peace but profound biological transformation."

Smiles of Compassion

"In the gentle curve of every little smile lies the power to touch the depths of somebody's heart, creating ripples of warmth that echo through the soul."

Sonnet of Hope

"The lullaby sweet of my heart unfolds, a sonnet written in the language of love, eternally sung to the rhythm of the soul, bearing the weight of dreams and the lightness of hope."

Soul's Voyage

"In the depths of soulful action, one finds the gentle current of joy, a river that carries the essence of our being towards fulfilment and purpose."

Symphony of the Spirit

"The universe is a grand chorus, and for those with the desire to sing, there's a song waiting to be uncovered—a harmonious expression of the spirit's unwavering journey."

The Art of Forgiveness

"Forgiveness is the gentle art of untangling the chains that bind your heart, freeing both yourself and others to find peace in the echoes of love."

The Art of Letting Go

"Letting go is not about giving up; it's about making space for something greater to enter your life."

The Dance of Release

"Decluttering is a dance of release; with every item we part with, we shed the weight of past attachments, allowing ourselves to embrace the present and all its possibilities."

The Elegance of Words

"Just as a finely crafted stitch enhances the allure of cloth, eloquent words embroider the canvas of life with the threads of beauty and meaning."

The Eternal Bliss Within

"True joy is untouched by the changing world; it lies within, in the divine bliss that requires no external validation. Once tasted, it satisfies like no earthly pleasure."

The Gift of Now

"To live in the moment is to release the past and not linger in the future. It is to recognize every breath as a blessing, and to savor the present with full awareness and gratitude."

The Journey of Self-Reflection

"Self-reflection is the quiet journey inward, where the heart meets its gaze, uncovering truths that guide us towards a more authentic and compassionate self."

The Mirror of Growth

"Through the lens of self-reflection, we see not just who we are, but who we are becoming—a mirror that reveals the beauty in our growth and the courage in our imperfections."

The Mystic's Sacred Language

"Silence is the sacred language of the mystics, a doorway to the infinite. In the stillness, we transcend the distractions of the outer world and awaken to the eternal presence within, discovering that true enlightenment begins not with sound, but with quietude."

The Power of Presence

"True peace is found not in escaping the present moment but in embracing it fully, with all its imperfections and beauty. In presence, we discover the timeless space where the soul resides."

The Radiance of the Soul

"When we turn within and see the divine light that resides in each of us, we begin to live as though we are already whole. This light never dims, even in our darkest hours."

The Reflective Nature of Silence

"Silence is a mirror, reflecting back the aspects of ourselves that we frequently ignore. In silence, we confront the depths of our desires, fears, and buried dreams, learning that beyond the commotion is the clarity to realise who we actually are."

The Sacred Path of Surrender

"Surrender is not a loss but a victory. It is the realisation that the greatest power lies not in resistance but in letting go of control and trusting the divine order."

The Silence Within

"In the silence of our hearts, we often find the answers we've been seeking in the noise of the world."

The Stillness of the Mind

"In the silence of a still mind, one finds the voice of truth. It speaks not in words but in a deep knowing that needs no explanation."

The Strength in Vulnerability

"Vulnerability is the birthplace of true courage. When we expose our hearts, we realise our true strength lies not in hiding but in the openness to be seen and loved as we are."

The Strength of Vulnerability

"In embracing our vulnerability, we discover the strength to be authentically ourselves."

Truly abundant life

"Happiness is not a destination reached through the accumulation of wealth, but a journey navigated with purpose and gratitude. It thrives in the fertile soil of contentment, where the seeds of kindness and fulfilment blossom into the vibrant flowers of a truly abundant life."

Union with the Divine

"The soul longs for union with the eternal, for a love that does not fade. In divine union, all earthly attachments fall away, leaving only the essence of pure, boundless love."

Unrestricted Thoughts

"Unchained and unrestricted thoughts become the architects of our deepest truths. The soul finds refuge in the freedom of thought, and the heart discovers the echoes of its most genuine desires."

Unshakable Peace

"To stand unshaken amidst life's storms is not the absence of struggle, but the mastery of peace. Like a mountain rising above the clouds, the soul that knows itself stands firm against all odds."

Unveiling Inner Beauty

"The journey to self-love is not about becoming someone else; it's about peeling away the layers of doubt and fear to uncover the beauty that has always been within you."

Wisdom in Balance

"Embrace the wisdom of life's equilibrium, where the strength of your efforts meets the serenity of surrender. The most profound music of your soul's symphony can be discovered in this balance."

The Power of Kindness

Spreading Compassion and Love

"Kindness is the quiet force that transforms the world, one small act at a time. It ripples through hearts, lighting the way for others to find compassion within themselves, creating a tapestry of love that binds us all together."

- *Shree Shambav*

A Journey to the Soul

"Silence is not an escape from the world, but a return to the soul—a journey where the deepest power is found in the space between words."

Awakening the Divine Within

"In the embrace of stillness, we awaken to the subtle whispers of the divine, revealing the profound presence that has always been within us."

Blooming Selflessness

"Unconditional love blooms when we give freely, expecting nothing in return; it is in this selflessness that we uncover life's deepest joys."

Broadening Horizons

"Perspectives shape our reality, but understanding transcends the limits of perception. By seeking to comprehend the stories and struggles of others, we broaden our horizons and cultivate deeper empathy."

Building Bridges of Connection

"Genuine understanding arises not from agreement, but from the willingness to listen, reflect, and embrace the complexity of different perspectives. It is through this process that we build bridges of connection and insight."

Catalyst for Healing and Renewal

"Silence is more than a sanctuary for the soul; it is a catalyst for the brain's healing and renewal. In the stillness, our minds recover from the barrage of overstimulation, allowing cognitive function to sharpen and emotional balance to be restored—proving that quiet isn't just soothing, it's essential for well-being."

Choosing Compassion Over Conflict

"The unkindness of others is a reflection of their struggles, not a reflection of your worth. Choose compassion over retaliation, for their actions belong to them alone. Protect your peace and integrity by refusing to let their negativity tarnish your spirit."

Compassion's Path

"With loving kindness as our compass and Ahimsa as our guiding principle, we navigate the intricate web of existence with gentleness and compassion, fostering a world where peace and harmony reign supreme."

Currency of Love

"Love, as a currency of the heart, is the most valuable investment in time. Wherever you go, spread its seeds generously, for lost moments of love are echoes that can never be retrieved."

Depths of Kindness

"In the depths of genuine kindness lies the willingness to relinquish one's necessities for the betterment of another, echoing the profound beauty of the human spirit."

Echoes of Forgiveness

"Beyond the noise of conflict, true victories resonate in the echoes of kindness and forgiveness. The battles that shape our destiny are not fought with weapons, but with the armour of compassion and the strength of a forgiving heart, forging a path to a triumphant and harmonious existence."

Embracing Freedom

"I harbour no competition within; I traverse my path, unbound by the urge to surpass others. My only ambition? To surpass my former self, for therein lies true freedom."

Embracing Loving Kindness and Ahimsa

"The essence of loving kindness and Ahimsa lies in recognising the interconnectedness of all life, weaving a tapestry of empathy and respect that honours the inherent dignity of every being."

Essence of Compassion

"The essence of kindness blooms when we offer what we cherish most, nurturing the seeds of compassion in the soil of selflessness."

Eternal Flame

"Love and compassion are the eternal flames that, when kindled within, not only brighten our path but radiate a warmth capable of thawing the coldest corners of the human soul."

From Suffering to Renewal

"Every painful experience is a charred ground waiting to turn green again. In the heart of suffering lies the seed of new beginnings, teaching us lessons that blossom into a life enriched by wisdom and strength."

Glow of Compassion

"In the gentle glow of compassion, hearts are kindled, and the warmth of love becomes a beacon, guiding us through the profound darkness of our shared humanity."

Healing Power of Forgiveness

"Forgiveness means embracing the tremendous power of healing. It is a brave act of self-love, providing solace to the wounded soul. Wounds are transformed into wisdom and scars into badges of strength in the soft embrace of forgiveness."

Healing Through Compassion

"A heart that speaks with compassion offers words that heal, turning wounds into wisdom and pain into purpose."

Hearing the Unsaid

"True listening goes beyond words; it is the art of hearing the unspoken emotions that linger in silence."

Illuminating Life with a Mother's Love

"The love of a mother is a flame that burns eternal, lighting the darkest corners of our existence with its radiant warmth."

Interdependence in Community

"The interconnectedness of the garden's plants mirrors the interdependence of community efforts, where each act of kindness supports the whole."

Journey of Redemption

"Through the delicate act of forgiving, we repair the damaged pieces of our souls. It is a sacred journey of redemption that demonstrates the strength of the human spirit. Forgiving permits us to let go of the weight of the past and embark on a brighter, more compassionate future."

Legacy of Hope and Kindness

"A true greatness is revealed when an old man plants a tree, knowing he will never sit in its shade, yet believing in the legacy of hope and kindness he leaves behind."

Measure of Kindness

"The true measure of kindness lies not in abundance, but in sacrifice. It's the act of offering a lantern of hope in the darkness, even when your path is dimly lit. For in giving a piece of yourself, you illuminate the world with the warmth of humanity's collective heart."

Melodies of the Heart

"The most profound melodies are concealed in the unspoken symphony of the human heart. Listen for the silent notes that resonate beyond the spoken words to understand another."

Noble Act of Forgiveness

"Forgiveness transcends the bounds of right and wrong; it's the noble act of choosing what is right for our souls."

Rebellion in Quietude

"In a world that glorifies noise, silence is a radical act of rebellion. It is in the quiet moments that we find the clarity to listen to our deepest truths, the wisdom to heal old wounds, and the strength to grow in ways the world's noise cannot nurture."

Rising Above Unkindness

"In the face of unkindness, hold fast to your kindness. Their actions are a reflection of their journey, not yours to carry. Choose to rise above bitterness and resentment, for your peace of mind is too precious to surrender to the wrongdoing of others."

Selfless Giving

"True kindness is the selfless act of giving when your own well runs dry. It's the willingness to offer a piece of your own heart, even when it means stitching yourself back together with tender threads of compassion."

Soothing Lullaby

"A soothing lullaby, a golden potion, as sweet as honey, an ethereal salve that calms the racing heart and transports it to the shores of peace."

Soulful Weavings

"In the tapestry of existence, words are the threads that weave the fabric of our souls. May we choose them with care, for every utterance carries the potential to either elevate the spirit or tarnish its essence. Let our speech be a reflection of the kindness and empathy that dwell within, nurturing the souls of both speaker and listener alike."

Strength in Inclusivity

"The beauty of perspectives lies in their diversity, and the strength of understanding lies in its inclusivity. When we open our minds to different viewpoints, we build bridges that connect us on the shared journey of humanity."

Strength in Togetherness

"Solidarity is not built on the foundation of knowledge alone but on the bonds of empathy and the collective will to stand together against adversity."

Tapestry of Love

"In the tapestry of life, Valentine's Day is the thread that reminds us of the profound significance of love, weaving together hearts with the gentle touch of affection and the resolute bond of commitment."

Tender Serenade

"In the tender notes of the lullaby sweet of my heart, echoes the timeless melody of love, a serenade that cradles dream and weaves the tapestry of enduring emotions."

The Bridge of Trust

"Integrity in listening is the promise that what is shared will be held with care, not scattered or betrayed."

The Bridge to Peace

"Forgiveness is the bridge that leads us from the darkness of anger to the light of peace, where we find our true selves waiting."

The Candle's Fragrant Sacrifice

"Good people are like candles, sacrificing themselves to bring light to others. Though their kindness may be overlooked or misused, the fragrance of their goodness spreads far and wide, creating beauty in unseen ways."

The Colors of Perception

"Though we share the same horizon, the colours we see are painted by our hopes, fears, and dreams."

The Courage to Be Present

"Authenticity in listening is not about perfect responses; it is about showing up fully, even when silence is all you have to offer."

The Echo of Empathy

"Kindness in speech is an echo that lingers long after the words are spoken, resonating in hearts and reshaping lives."

The Echo of Goodness

"Life is an echo; the goodness you invest in the world will always find its way back to you. Rather than seeking success alone, strive to do good, for in kindness lies the true reward of the soul."

The essence of Silence

"The true essence of a soul lies not in the words it speaks, but in the profound silence that holds the unspoken, revealing a depth untouched by mere conversation."

The Essence of True Justice

"True justice is not blind to the entirety of a person's life; it sees beyond mere mistakes, delving into the depths of their character to weigh the balance between faults and virtues. In the scales of justice, the weight of good deeds holds equal significance, for fairness can only emerge when the whole truth is embraced, not just fragments of it."

The Garden of Connection

"Listening with honesty, authenticity, integrity, and love is like tending a garden—each conversation is a seed that blooms into understanding."

The Gentle Rain of Kindness

"Kindness in words is a gentle rain; it refreshes the weary, nurtures trust, and transforms even the hardest ground into fertile soil for understanding."

The Gift of Presence

"When you listen with your heart instead of your ears, you offer a gift that words alone can never match."

The Harmony of Heartfelt Wins

"Winning against rivals may bring trophies, but winning hearts fills life with purpose, joy, and lasting harmony."

The Heart's Eye

"Eyes capture the surface, but it's the heart that reveals the world's true beauty, hidden beyond what sight alone can hold."

The Heart's Silent Truths

"In the quiet embrace of stillness, the heart speaks truths the world cannot hear, unlocking the strength we've always carried within."

The Language of Love

"Love transforms listening from an act of hearing into an act of healing—it says, You matter. I am here for you."

The Lasting Impression of Love

"Gentle words are like footprints in the sands of memory—soft, enduring, and impossible to erase."

The Light of Kindness

"When words are spoken with kindness, they become beacons of hope, illuminating paths in the darkest of times."

The Lightness of Forgiveness

"Forgiveness is the gentle act of setting down the burdens that weigh upon our hearts, allowing us to walk lighter and breathe deeper."

The Mirror of Truth

"Honesty in listening is like a clear mirror—it reflects the speaker's truth, unclouded by the fog of your assumptions."

The Power of Gentle Words

"A single kind word can mend what a thousand harsh ones could destroy; it is the seed of peace in a garden of discord."

The Power of Stillness

"In a world that shouts, listening is the quiet revolution that builds bridges where words cannot."

The Presence of Self

"Silence is not the absence of sound, but the presence of self. It is the sacred space where the chaos of life falls away, allowing us to reconnect with the forgotten rhythm of our own being, to find peace amidst the clamour, and to remember who we truly are."

The Price of Riches

"In the pursuit of worldly treasures, one must tread cautiously, for what value lies in amassing all the riches of the earth if it costs the essence of one's soul? True wealth transcends material abundance, found instead in the depths of compassion, integrity, and inner peace."

The Sacred Space of Stillness

"Stillness is the sacred space where the noise of the world fades, allowing us to connect with the divine presence that guides our hearts and illuminates our path."

The Sanctuary of True Listening

"Listening is not the act of hearing words; it is the art of hearing souls. When you listen with honesty, authenticity, integrity, and love, you become a sanctuary where the unspoken is revealed, and hearts are healed."

The Timeless Impact of Kindness

"Words may fade and actions may pass, but the imprint of how you made someone feel lingers eternally in their heart. Choose kindness, empathy, and authenticity, for these are the timeless gifts that resonate beyond words and deeds."

The Triumph of Connection

"True triumph lies not in defeating others, but in inspiring loyalty, trust, and love in those who stand beside us."

The Wealth of Generosity

"In the act of giving, we unlock the boundless potential of our hearts, for true richness resides not in what we possess, but in the generosity, we bestow upon others."

Transforming Inner Landscapes

"Through the practice of stillness, we cultivate the awareness of a divine presence, transforming our inner landscape into a sanctuary of peace and connection."

Triumph of Kindness

"In the grand tapestry of life, victories are not won on the battlegrounds of wars and confrontation. True triumph emerges from the fertile soil of kindness and forgiveness—a garden where the seeds of compassion yield a harvest of enduring peace."

True Love's Vision

"True love sees beyond flaws; it embraces imperfections and cherishes the uniqueness that resides within each of us."

Unity Beyond Knowledge

"Solidarity does not depend on what we know, but on the shared compassion and unwavering support we extend to one another in times of need."

Unlocking Inner Power

"Amid the whispers of silence, we find not the absence of sound, but the presence of our true self—an inner power waiting to be unlocked through stillness."

Valentine's Thread

"On Valentine's Day, we celebrate not just love, but the enduring power of connection and the beauty of shared moments that transcend time and space."

Victory in Life's True Game

"Victory in a game is earned by outplaying opponents; victory in life is won by uplifting the hearts around us."

Vision Beyond Sight

"Two eyes see the world, yet no two hearts perceive it the same; for vision rests not in sight alone, but in the depths of one's soul."

Whisper of Compassion

"Forgiveness is the gentle whisper of compassion, urging us to embrace what is just and honourable, regardless of the surrounding chaos."

Whispers of the Divine

Cosmic connection

"When we quiet the mind and listen to the whispers of the Divine, we feel the pulse of the universe within us, a reminder that our souls are forever intertwined with the cosmic dance of creation, forever part of something infinitely greater than ourselves."

- *Shree Shambav*

A Gentle Breeze of Change

"He came into our lives quietly, like a gentle breeze, and left us forever changed. His legacy is the wisdom and compassion we carry forward."

A Harmonious Bond

"By honoring my energy, I forge a harmonious bond, where each act of self-care is mirrored by the universe's gentle embrace."

Aching Loss

"To lose someone dear is to endure a profound ache that reverberates through the very core of our being, reminding us of the irreplaceable imprint they've left on our lives."

Alignment with the Divine

"Learning to accept whatever comes our way, while still putting forth our best efforts, aligns us with the will of the Divine."

Awakening Joy

"Like the gentle rays of the morning sun kissing the earth awake, self-love awakens the dormant seeds of happiness within us, casting out the shadows of doubt and filling our hearts with the warmth of acceptance and contentment."

Awareness in Life's Symphony

"In life's intricate dance, awareness serves as the rhythm that orchestrates pain and pleasure into a harmonious symphony of existence."

Blossoming Joy

"In the sacred garden of the now, joy reveals itself as a vibrant bloom waiting to be plucked, its fragrant whispers echoing the profound truth that life's exquisite beauty resides within the fabric of each transient moment."

Celestial Clarity and Purpose

"Through the nurturing of virtues, the higher soul's light permeates our being, steering the incarnated soul and body with celestial clarity and purpose."

Cherishing the Richness of Everyday Moments

"In the whispers of laughter, the warmth of a shared glance, and the sweetness of a quiet sunset, lies the treasure trove of life's truest riches. Embrace each fleeting moment with gratitude, for it is in these small fragments that happiness blooms brightest."

Cherishing the Sacredness of Each Moment

"To live with the awareness of our mortality is to cherish the sacredness of each moment, making our existence a continuous celebration."

Cosmic Ballet

"Spirituality, often misunderstood, is the silent whisper of an inner science—a science untethered from the tangible threads of the physical world. It's the delicate dance of unseen forces that have existed since the dawn of time. In this cosmic ballet, science and spirituality interweave to create a tapestry that goes beyond empirical understanding and penetrates into the mysteries of the soul."

Dancing in the Present Moment

"Living fully in the present moment is like dancing in the rain, where every drop is a chance to feel alive and connected to the rhythm of the universe."

Depths of Reflection

"When we reflect deeply, reality reveals its deep mysteries, beckoning us to look below the surface and find the hidden truths that illuminate the path of wisdom."

Divine Crafting

"Designed by the divine, the softness of heart and tongue becomes the crucible where the almighty blends the purest ingredients of empathy, compassion, and kindness, crafting a recipe for a life rich in the sweetest and most enduring flavors."

Echoes of Endless Love

"Like the gentle caress of a familiar melody, love permeates the soul, leaving behind a trail of resonant chords that linger in the heart long after the song has ended, a timeless echo of the soul's connection."

Echoes of Eternal Union

"In the tender embrace of surrender, we find the raw beauty of union, where the river's every ripple becomes a whispered confession of belonging. Just as the river unveils its eternal unity with the boundless ocean, so too does the soul, in sacred surrender, unveil its timeless connection to the Divine. It is a metamorphosis of profound grace, where the self dissolves into the infinite, and in that dissolution, discovers the ineffable depth of its eternal oneness with the Divine, an eternal symphony that echoes through the very fabric of existence."

Echoes of Gratitude

"Amidst the verdant tapestry of creation, we are but humble recipients of nature's boundless generosity, cradled in the embrace of ancient trees and serenaded by the melodies of the wild. Only in moments of quiet reflection do we realise the depth of our indebtedness to the earth, igniting a fervent resolve to protect and cherish its splendour for the generations yet to come."

Echoes of Truth

"In the quiet depths of solitude, the soul whispers its most profound truths, echoing the timeless wisdom that resides within each of us, awaiting our silent contemplation."

Embracing Life's Lessons

"When we embrace every moment, whether joyful or painful, we learn that life's greatest lessons come from the most unexpected places."

Embracing Pain with Awareness

"Life's ultimate bliss and divinity unfold not in avoiding pain, but in embracing it with profound awareness, allowing it to metamorphose into wisdom."

Embracing Resilience and Clarity

"In the stillness of my solitude, I embraced the quiet whispers of change, and in doing so, I discovered a depth of resilience and clarity that reshaped my entire being. This profound shift illuminated a path of compassion and strength, guiding me toward a more authentic and enlightened existence."

Embracing the Depths of Existence

"Like the young fish yearning to explore the ocean's depths, we too harbour dreams that stretch beyond the horizon of our imagination. Yet, it is only through the gentle guidance of love and the embrace of wisdom that we come to understand the preciousness of what lies within and around us. Let us dive fearlessly into the waters of our souls, propelled by the currents of curiosity and gratitude, and emerge enlightened by the profound beauty of our interconnectedness with all creation."

Essence of Spirituality

"Spirituality transcends the confines of religion, meditation, and yoga; it is the sacred essence that infuses every moment of our existence. It is the profound connection to the cosmos, the whisper of the soul, guiding us along the path of inner transformation and awakening."

Eternal Anthem

"Beyond the pages of scriptures, Lord Rama's saga breathes with the heartbeat of humanity. His love, sacrifice, and unwavering commitment to truth etch a profound narrative on the canvas of our hearts. In the symphony of existence, Rama's melody is a timeless anthem, echoing the eternal call to live a life anchored in virtue."

Eternal Reverberations

"Within the sacred dialogue between mortal and Divine, every word uttered carries the weight of eternity, weaving a tapestry of wisdom and grace that transcends the boundaries of time and space, illuminating the depths of our being with celestial light."

Eternity in Moments

"In the fleeting dance of time, we find eternity captured within the delicate folds of moments, each verse a testament to the timeless beauty of existence."

Everyday Sacredness

"Every moment can be sacred if we choose to see its inherent beauty and significance."

Finding Beauty in the Present

"In the ebb and flow of life's currents, we often overlook the treasures that lie within our grasp, blinded by the allure of distant horizons. It is only when we pause to listen to the whispers of our hearts that we realise the depth of our connection to the world around us, and the beauty that surrounds us in every moment."

Finding Strength in the Silence of Prayer

"In the echoes of silent prayers, where tears meet the stars, we find the courage to embrace our vulnerabilities and the strength to rise from the ashes of despair."

Finding Wealth in Surrender

"In the darkness of loss, we find the light of surrender, realising that true wealth lies not in possessions, but in the embrace of the Divine."

Flowing with Life

"When we release our fears of the future, we step into the flow of life, trusting that the river will carry us to exactly where we need to be."

Foundation of Hope and Resilience

"The enduring power of his teachings has become our foundation, guiding us toward a future filled with hope and resilience."

Gateway to Transformation

"Within the embrace of personal change lies the gateway to profound spiritual transformation."

Guided by the Wisdom of Life's Currents

"Just as the young turtle finds solace in the embrace of the ocean's guidance, so too can we discover our path by connecting with the essence of the world. Our destiny is not merely a destination but a journey of profound self-discovery and growth."

Guiding Young Souls through the Cosmos

"In the vast expanse of existence, each person is a unique constellation, twinkling with their own brilliance against the canvas of the cosmos. Embrace them as they are, with all their quirks and imperfections, for it is in this acceptance that a true connection is forged. With patience as your compass, kindness as your guiding star, and tolerance as your beacon of light, illuminate the path for young souls to find their place in the universe."

Harmony Between Heart and Mind

"In the dance of life, let the heart lead with its wisdom of compassion and intuition, and allow the mind to follow with its clarity and discernment. Together, they create harmony and purpose."

Harmony in Existence

"In the delicate dance of existence, the preservation of ecosystems emerges as the cornerstone of our collective resilience and prosperity. Beyond safeguarding biodiversity, it nurtures the roots of physical vitality, fosters emotional resilience, cultivates mental clarity, and fosters the bonds that bind communities together in a tapestry of shared purpose and interconnectedness."

Harmony of Prayers

"In the symphony of life, our prayers echo silently, each a plea for understanding, for belonging, for hope. Through tears and longing, in the depths of despair, we find solace in the realisation that our hearts beat as one, united by the silent whispers of faith, weaving a tapestry of compassion and resilience in the vast expanse of existence."

Harmony Unveiled

"In the gentle embrace of nature's symphony, we find echoes of our own soul's yearning for connection, reminding us that our well-being is intertwined with the delicate dance of the earth's ecosystems."

Harmony Unveiled

"Within the embrace of nature's symphony, we find ourselves woven into the fabric of existence, enveloped by the gentle whispers of leaves and the resounding chorus of life. Yet, in our haste, we risk overlooking the profound interconnectedness that sustains us, failing to grasp the sacredness of each fluttering wing and rustling branch."

Harmony with Life's Flow

"This acceptance is not resignation, but an understanding and harmony with life's natural flow, embodying the essence of true yoga."

Illuminating Darkness Through Prayer

"In the silent whispers of prayer, amidst tears of anguish and longing, we discover the profound truth that in our darkest moments, the light of hope shines brightest."

Illuminating the Path of Fulfilment

"In the acts of service and tithing, the soul shines brightest, illuminating the path to spiritual fulfilment and profound inner peace."

Illuminating the Path of Purpose

"With a heart unburdened by doubt and a mind clear as a mountain stream, the path ahead becomes illuminated by the light of purpose."

Journey of Awakening

"Awakening is not an event but a journey of deepening consciousness, where every moment becomes a portal to infinite wisdom."

Journey of Consciousness

"To unravel the intricacies of existence, one must embark on a journey of profound reflection, traversing the vast expanse of consciousness to grasp the essence of reality in its purest form."

Journey of Oneness

"Unlocking the door to oneness requires relinquishing the shackles of limiting ideas and breaking free from the chains of lower emotions. To attain harmony with your higher self, embark on the profound journey of building your character—a transformative odyssey where the echoes of authenticity resonate with the symphony of your soul."

Journey to the Heart of Discovery

"Within the depths of seeking lies the treasure trove of discovery, where earnest hearts uncover the riches of wisdom, purpose, and truth amidst life's intricate tapestry."

Krishna's Call

"Krishna's guidance becomes a powerful call to inner peace and resilience, urging us to embrace the ebb and flow of life's ocean with a steadfast heart and an even mind."

Listening to the Whispers Within

"Learn to listen to the whispers of your heart, for it holds the essence of your true desires and passions. Let the mind serve as a loyal companion, translating dreams into plans with clarity and purpose."

Living by His Principles

"We took too long to understand him, but now we must live by the principles he graced upon us, for his teachings are the true treasures he left behind."

Meditative Growth

"From meditation grows silence, serenity, and sensitivity, enriching every aspect of life."

Melody of Creation

"In the eternal dance of existence, creation unfolds as a continuous melody, orchestrating the symphony of life with each fleeting note."

Nature's Verses

"Nature whispers its eternal verses through the rustling leaves, each word a testament to the profound love story between Earth and all its living creatures."

Navigating Chaos

"Amidst the chaos of existence, clarity illuminates the path, purity nourishes the soul, and intention guides the way to boundless fulfilment."

Nurturing the Soul

"The soul's growth is nurtured in the fertile ground of pain and pleasure, each experience a step toward transcendence."

Ocean of Grace

"The ocean of grace is a symbol of God's never-ending love, a vast, deep, and unfailing love."

Path of Responsibility

"Choosing to walk the path of spiritual evolution means accepting the great responsibility of seeing the subtleties of life clearly and acting with grace in accordance with your actions."

Path to Spiritual Growth

"Embracing personal change is the path to spiritual growth, illuminating the journey within."

Paving the Path to Inner Freedom

"The path to inner freedom is paved with the stones we lay down—the resentments forgiven, the fears released, the moments embraced with gratitude."

Pinnacle of Wisdom

"To truly know others is a mark of intelligence, but to truly know oneself is the pinnacle of wisdom, where the depths of our soul meet the vast expanse of the universe."

Pursuit of Enlightenment

"We learn about others through the pursuit of knowledge; we explore the depths of our own being through the pursuit of enlightenment."

Rama's Triumph

"Lord Rama, the celestial architect of dharma, weaves his story into the fabric of our souls. His trials and triumphs echo through the corridors of time, resonating with the universal chord that binds humanity, teaching us that the true victory lies in upholding principles over power."

Resonance of Connection

"A soul finds its deepest resonance in the ebb and flow of connection; let love be the thread that binds, but leave space for the winds of the heavens to whisper their secrets."

Ripples of Humanity

"In the vast ocean of existence, every soul is but a ripple, intertwining with others in the grand symphony of life, reminding us that within our connections lie the essence of our humanity."

Rooted Resilience

"Amidst the chaos of modernity, let us not forget that our roots lie in the embrace of the natural world. Our future, and the legacy we leave for generations to come, depends on our ability to cherish, protect, and restore the delicate balance of ecosystems with reverence and love."

Rooted Spiritual Growth

"True spiritual growth begins with the honest appraisal of life's intricacies, leading to actions rooted in wisdom, compassion, and authenticity."

Sacred Confluence

"In the gentle embrace of surrender, we find the profound truth just as the river becomes one with the boundless ocean, so too does the soul merge with the Divine. In this sacred union, we discover not only our eternal oneness, but the beauty of our existence as a shimmering reflection of the infinite."

Sacred Stewardship

"The preservation of ecosystems is more than just a duty; it's a sacred covenant with the future, a pledge to protect the sanctity of life in all its forms. Our stewardship of the environment reverberates through time, shaping the physical, emotional, and mental landscapes of generations yet to come, and sowing the seeds of profound connection and enduring well-being."

Sanctity of Spiritual Bond

"Within the sanctity of a strong spiritual bond, love intertwines with kindness, empathy flows effortlessly, power arises from compassion, and clarity emerges as the harmonious symphony of the soul's deepest truths."

Shared Spirituality

"Temples and ceremonies are gateways to connect with the spiritual experiences of our ancestors."

Soulful Resilience

"Soulful resilience is born in the crucible of hardship, where the fires of suffering mould spirits into monuments of strength, and scars become eloquent stories of endurance."

Soulful Resonance

"In the silent spaces between heartbeats, amidst the ethereal echoes, we find reflections that transcend the limitations of language, speaking directly to the depths of our being, where emotions and truths intertwine in a dance of soulful resonance."

Symphony of Spiritual Connection

"In the profound depths of spiritual connection, love becomes the guiding force, kindness the natural expression, empathy the bridge between souls, power the gentle strength to uplift, and clarity the unwavering beacon illuminating the path of purpose."

Tapestry of Wisdom and Grace

"As virtues flourish within us, the higher soul weaves a tapestry of wisdom and grace, guiding the incarnated soul and body toward divine harmony."

The Completeness of Each Moment

"When we live with awareness, the future becomes unnecessary, for each moment is lived so completely that nothing is left wanting."

The Harmony of Embrace

"In the house of the spirit, we must let in both the friend and the enemy, for it is through this embrace that we find true harmony."

The Path to Profound Joy

"Only by moving through suffering can we open the door to profound joy, for it is the contrast that illuminates our path to enlightenment."

The Preciousness of Every Moment

"Between each breath lies the fragile boundary of life and death, a reminder of our transient existence and the preciousness of every moment."

The Promise of a New Beginning

"To let go is to acknowledge the past without letting it define our future, and to trust that each moment holds the promise of a new beginning."

The Quiet Truth of Existence

"In the stillness between breaths, we find the quiet truth of life and death, a profound silence that speaks to the essence of our being."

The Sanctuary Within

"In tending to my energy, I create a sanctuary within, where vitality and peace flourish, reciprocating my care with boundless grace."

The Soul's Voice in Service and Tithing

"Through service and tithing, the soul finds its voice, expressing love, compassion, and generosity in a world yearning for connection."

The Space for Unexpected Blessings

"In the absence of what you desired lies the space for unexpected blessings to bloom, revealing paths of resilience, wisdom, and new beginnings."

Threads of Wisdom

"In the tapestry of enlightenment, sometimes the threads of wisdom are woven in the dance of an old man, revealing that the true master is found where the heart listens and the soul dances."

Transcending Dualities

"Maturity is not just about growing older but about expanding our consciousness, embracing life's dualities, and transcending them."

Transformative Evolution

"In the crucible of suffering, strength, wisdom, and compassion are forged, birthing a transformative evolution of the soul that emerges resilient and enlightened."

Transforming Moments with Awareness

"True awareness and gratitude transform every experience into a lesson, every moment into a treasure, leading us to welcome death with open arms."

Turning Towards the Light

"Our regrets and worries are the shadows of life, but when we turn towards the light of the present, they dissolve, revealing the beauty of now."

Uniting Hearts in Life's Symphony

"In the tapestry of life, woven with threads of longing and faith, echoes of two prayers converge into one heartbeat, teaching us that amidst life's trials, it's in the embrace of compassion and the light of faith where the truest miracles are found."

Unveiling Authenticity

"True transformation begins when we courageously peel away the layers of falsehood, revealing the radiant core of our authentic selves beneath."

Unveiling Pure Awareness

"To awaken is to unveil that beyond the veil of suffering and joy lies the essence of pure awareness, the genesis of all experience."

Valleys of Awakening

"Awakening is not on the distant mountain; it's in the quiet valleys where the soul resonates with the melodies of life's profound wisdom."

Verses in the Heart

"Amidst the transient whispers of life, we carve eternity in the heart's sacred chambers, where memories linger like verses etched in the fabric of eternity."

Walking with Reverence

"To live sensitively is to walk with reverence, knowing that each encounter with nature reveals a new facet of the divine."

Waves of Mercy

"In the ocean of grace, there is always enough for everyone, and the waves of mercy never stop flowing."

Way of Life

"Beyond the rituals and practices lies the true essence of spirituality—a way of life woven with threads of compassion, gratitude, and self-awareness. It is the journey of the heart, where each step taken with intention becomes a pilgrimage towards the divine within."

Weaving Destiny's Threads

"As virtues blossom within, the soul's tendrils reach ever deeper into the fabric of existence, intertwining with the threads of fate to shape the course of life's journey, forging a bond between the celestial and the corporeal, where the spirit reigns supreme."

Whispers of the Divine

"In the quiet expanse of the soul, amidst the whispers of the wind and the silent dance of stars, we find ourselves engaged in celestial conversations, where the Divine speaks in the language of the heart, guiding us on the path of enlightenment and understanding."

Wings of Possibility

"In the realm of the impossible, the blessings of the Guru and the grace of the divine are the sacred keys that unlock the gates of possibility. With faith as your compass and surrender as your guide, even the loftiest dreams find wings to soar."

Wisdom from the Ages

Timeless Insights for Life

"Timeless wisdom does not seek to explain life, but to remind us that within every challenge, there is a lesson, within every hardship, there is strength, and that true growth comes from embracing the journey, not the destination."

- *Shree Shambav*

Becoming the Promise

"Integrity is not just about keeping promises; it's about becoming the promise—a living testament to the truth we profess."

The Bridge of Trust

"Integrity is the bridge between words and actions—a path where trust walks hand in hand with truth."

The Mastery of Freedom

"To act without attachment is to free oneself from the chains of expectation; it is in this freedom that true mastery of the self is found."

Beauty in Experience and Guidance

"To understand the value of elders is to see the beauty in their experiences, the purity in their hearts, and the strength in their silent guidance."

Beauty of Compassion

"Gaze beyond the façade, where true beauty reveals itself not in the contours of a face but in the luminosity that emanates from the depths of a compassionate heart."

Beyond Faults

"To achieve true justice, we must abandon the narrow confines of judgment based solely on flaws and missteps. Instead, we must widen our perspective to embrace the full spectrum of an individual's character—their kindness, their compassion, their contributions to the world. In this holistic view, the scale of justice finds equilibrium, recognising that a person's worth is not measured by their faults alone but by the entirety of their being."

Beyond the Cover

"In the book of Life, many glance at the cover, some explore the prologue, and a few critique the chapters. But it is the rare souls who immerse themselves in the narrative, discovering the essence of our being."

Brilliance of Life's Colours

"Without the wisdom of elders, our lives are like a butterfly without its brilliant colours, a peacock without its dance."

Collective Strength

"Alone, our impact may seem insignificant, but together, we possess the strength to create profound change."

Compassionate Embrace

"To be truly compassionate is to hold another's sorrow as if it were your own, with a heart wide open to healing."

Depths of Understanding

"In the depths of understanding others, we find intelligence; in the depths of understanding ourselves, we find true wisdom."

Earth's Ancient Wisdom

"In every rustling leaf and flowing river, the Earth whispers ancient truths, urging us to listen and learn from the wisdom woven into its very fabric."

Embrace the Pain

"In our efforts to avoid pain, we inadvertently avoid the depths of our true selves. Embrace the pain because it leads to a deeper understanding of who you are beyond the shadows of suffering."

Embracing Cycles

"Embrace the cycles of your life; just as nature sheds leaves to make way for new blooms, we too must release the past to welcome new beginnings."

Embracing Life's Dance

"In the ephemeral dance of life, we are akin to butterflies, fragile yet resilient. To hold onto moments too tightly is to suffocate their fleeting beauty, but to embrace them with gentle reverence is to witness their graceful flight. In the delicate balance between presence and release, we learn the profound art of living fully and letting go."

Eroding the Bonds of Trust

"Honesty is not merely the absence of deceit; it is the presence of integrity. It is the bridge upon which trust walks, transforming conversations into connections and hearts into homes."

Eternal Treasure

"In the realm of existence, wealth fades and fortunes shift, but knowledge stands eternal, an unyielding treasure that enriches the soul and brightens the path of life."

Eternity's Embrace

"Within the intricate tapestry of time, the past whispers its secrets, the future beckons with possibilities, and the present, a fleeting moment where all eternity resides."

Grace in Gratitude

"In the ephemeral moments of life, where time stands still, we find grace in gratitude—a gentle reminder that even the smallest blessings can illuminate our path."

Guiding Stars

"As we navigate the boundless darkness of existence, passions become the guiding stars, casting their luminous glow on the intricate map of our journey, revealing the way to purpose and fulfilment."

Harmony of Existence

"Amidst the ebb and flow of existence, we find solace in the harmony of light illuminating our path and shadows guiding our introspection."

Harmony of Insight and Deed

"True wisdom lies in the unity of thought and deed, for the wise know that knowledge without action is incomplete, and action without knowledge is blind."

Harmony of Strength

"True strength is not found in the muscles of the body alone, but in the harmony between a healthy body and a serene mind."

Home's Heart and Wisdom

"The presence of elders transforms a house into a home, filling it with warmth, wisdom, and unwavering support."

Lessons from Detours

"Life's greatest lessons often come from the unexpected detours we take on our journey."

Life's Hidden Treasure

"Amid the vast expanse of the ocean, the fish swims, oblivious to the priceless wonders that envelop it. Such is life, where often, the most precious treasures lie hidden in the everyday currents of our existence."

Love's Script

"In the grand theatre of existence, let love be the script you unfold wherever you go. Lost time, once squandered, leaves a void that can never be filled again."

Mastering the Flame

"Either you control your anger, or it controls the fire in your soul."

Moments of Aliveness

"In the end, it is not the milestones we remember, but the moments we felt most alive."

Nature's Cycles of Growth

"Nature speaks in cycles, reminding us that growth comes from patience and resilience, teaching us to embrace the seasons of our own lives."

Pain as Artistry

"Amidst the maya world's twists and turns, pain becomes the artist's tool, etching a masterpiece that unveils the beauty hidden within the human experience."

Parenthood's Privilege

"In the sacred dance of parenthood, remember this truth your children are not extensions of your identity, but embodiments of Life's relentless quest for expression. They emerge through the tapestry of your existence, a testament to Life's creative pulse. Embrace the privilege of witnessing their journey, for in their autonomy, they discover the symphony of their own purpose."

Peaceful Resolution

"True forgiveness isn't about proving who's right or wrong; it's about finding peace in doing what's right, regardless of the circumstances."

Power of Unity

"The true strength lies not in individual endeavours but in the collective force that emerges when hearts and hands join together."

Recognising Immeasurable Depth

"To honour the legacy of our elders is to recognise the immeasurable depth of their sacrifices and dedication."

Steadfast Character

"Reputation may be a fleeting shadow, dancing in the light of public opinion, but character stands as the unwavering lighthouse, guiding your journey through the storms of life."

The Beauty of Closure

"In the gentle embrace of reflection, we find that closure is not an end but a new beginning, revealing the beauty woven into the fabric of our imperfections."

The Chain of Command

"Anger is a wild beast—either you tame it, or it will cage you."

The Choice of Power

"When anger leads, you follow blindly; when you lead, anger becomes powerless."

The Cost of Deception

"Dishonesty may offer a momentary comfort, but its cost is the slow erosion of the very trust that binds us to each other."

The Dance of Grace

"Grace dances in the quiet corners of our existence, whispering the profound truth that every fleeting moment is an invitation to appreciate the beauty that surrounds us."

The Fragility of Scattered Secrets

"To trust someone with your secrets is to gift them a piece of your soul. When they scatter these pieces carelessly, it speaks volumes about their own fragility and the hollowness of their commitments."

The Freedom of Forgiveness

"To forgive is to release the weight of the past, freeing both ourselves and those we hold captive in our memories."

The Garden of the Mind

"The mind is a garden, and the body its soil; tend to the soil with care, and the garden will flourish with peace."

The Growth of Love

"The heart's capacity to love is infinite, but it is in the giving that it truly learns to grow."

The Language of Kindness

"Kindness is a silent language, speaking in gestures of the heart and leaving warmth wherever it goes."

The Lens of Gratitude

"Gratitude turns what we have into enough, and more—it's the lens through which we see the abundance in every moment."

The Masterpiece of the Journey

"The journey teaches us that every step, every stumble, is a brushstroke in the masterpiece of our lives; true peace lies in embracing the whole, not just the finished work."

The Measure of a Life

"The measure of a life well-lived is not in the years we accumulate, but in the love we give and the kindness we leave behind."

The Melody of Wellness

"In the quiet rhythm of a healthy body, the mind finds its song—a melody of peace, clarity, and inner joy."

The Path of Integrity

"To speak the truth with kindness is not just to convey facts, but to illuminate the path for others, leading them through the shadows of doubt into the light of understanding."

The Power of Truth

"Honesty is not just the absence of lies; it is the presence of clarity, the willingness to share what is real, and the courage to be vulnerable in the face of it."

The Price of Ignored Wisdom

"Regret is the shadow of ignored wisdom; trust your heart before it's too late."

The Sacred Legacy of Books

"Books are the silent guardians of civilization, condensed reservoirs of centuries' worth of human experience. Within their pages, we find the wisdom of ages distilled, offering solace, guidance, and profound insights. They stand as the most patient of teachers, the wisest of counselors, accessible to all who seek their knowledge. To immerse oneself in the reading of fine books is to engage in a dialogue with the finest minds of history, whose words leave indelible footprints upon the sands of time."

The Seasons of Life

"Life unfolds like the seasons: each phase a chapter of growth, reminding us that even in winter, the promise of spring lies beneath the surface."

The Seed of Trust

"Trust is not built on perfect words, but on the honesty behind them—when the heart speaks the truth, the soul listens and believes."

The Soul's Reflection

"True beauty is seen not with the eyes, but felt with the soul—a reflection of the light we carry within."

The Surface and Depth of Life

"Our life is like a book; most people view only the cover. Few delve into the prologue, some make an effort with the introduction, many critique its content, but only a handful truly read and understand the story within."

The Swift Betrayal

"Trust is the foundation of friendship; never place it in the hands of those who betray others' secrets, for they will betray yours just as swiftly."

The Temple of the Spirit

"The body is the temple in which the spirit resides; nourish it with love, and the spirit will dance in the light of inner peace."

The Tenuous Thread of Democracy

"Democracy hangs by a tenuous thread, woven from the hopes and voices of the people, demanding our unwavering dedication to keep it from unravelling."

The Weight of Silence

"Silence holds the weight of emotions unspoken, revealing the beauty of connection that transcends words, allowing us to feel what is often left unsaid."

The Weight of Silence

"Sometimes, silence is more truthful than words. It carries the weight of what cannot yet be said, until the right moment and the right intention arise."

The Whisper of Dawn and Dusk

"In the quiet moments between dawn and dusk, life whispers the lessons of time, urging us to embrace every heartbeat. As the days turn into memories, time reveals the profound value of each fleeting second, reminding us that the essence of life is found in the moments we often take for granted."

The Whisper of Inner Truth

"Listen to your inner voice—it whispers the truths the world is too loud to hear."

Threads of Beauty

"Like a masterful stitch embellishes fabric, the right words intricately weave beauty into the tapestry of life."

Touches of Selfless Sacrifice

"From cradle to grave, every moment we live is touched by the selfless sacrifices of those who came before us."

Transcending Boundaries

"Life's pursuit of escape is not a call for sacrifice; it's a plea to transcend the boundaries of fear, pain, and the silent struggles of enduring suffering."

Treasures of the Overlooked

"In the hurried world, we miss life's quiet treasures; it's the overlooked joys that nourish our hearts and keep us whole."

Unity of Knowledge and Action

"In the eyes of the wise, knowledge and action are inseparable threads woven into the fabric of truth. Only by embracing both can we truly see and understand the world."

Unveiled Stories

"Behind every mask lies a story untold, for it is in the depths of our true selves that our greatest triumphs and vulnerabilities reside."

Unveiling the Soul

"The pain we fear is not a stranger; it is the echo of experiences already lived. To feel it completely is not to endure more, but to unveil the vastness of our being that transcends the limits of suffering. Embrace your pain, for within its crucible, you discover the richness of your soul."

Unveiling Truth

"In the dance of life, truth wears a cloak of metaphors, obscured by desire and dust. Only through introspection can we unveil the wisdom that lies beneath the veils of existence."

Weight of Absence

"In the silent spaces between breaths, the weight of absence presses heavy upon the heart, reminding us that some departures leave behind wounds that time alone cannot heal."

Whispered Epiphanies

"The most profound notes in the symphony of existence are the whispers of silent epiphanies. They reverberate within our hearts, revealing the timeless truths that guide our steps on this cosmic dance floor known as life."

Whispers of the Soul

"In the stillness of silence, we discover the truths our hearts yearn to express; it is in these moments that we truly listen to the whispers of our souls."

Life Coach and Philanthropist

Shree Shambav is the visionary founder of the Shree Shambav Ayur Rakshita Foundation (www.shambav-ayurrakshita.org). He founded this institution with a lofty goal: to recognise human identity across gender, ethnicity, and nationality. Through this organisation, he wants to assist all communities in realising their full potential and the intrinsic beauty of life.

Shree Shambav, a Life Coach, is dedicated to supporting people on their journeys of self-discovery and empowerment. He assists people in discovering who they are, determining what inspires and drives them, and overcoming limiting ideas. His approach clarifies what one wants in life, assisting people through goal-setting and a step-by-step process for achieving them. He empowers people to make deliberate and responsible decisions, allowing them to identify their blind spots and evolve as individuals via the use of numerous strategies and tools.

The foundation's bold, uncompromising, and compassionate ventures are always aimed at initiating the "Inner Transformation" process. They focus on spiritual growth, personal growth, and self-healing while emphasising that true progress lies in "Inclusive Growth and Co-existence." This philosophy drives all their initiatives, encouraging a holistic approach to development and well-being.

Under Shree Shambav's leadership, the foundation has launched several impactful movements:

Shree Shambav Green Movement: This mission is to create a healthy, green, and clean earth through responsible water conservation and greening initiatives. The movement strives to make the world a green paradise by encouraging sustainable living and environmental responsibility.

Shree Shambav Vidya Vedhika (Vizhuthugal): This project aims to help students and children by offering training, books, stationery, and uniforms. It aims to provide the next generation with the tools and resources they need to excel both academically and personally.

Shree Shambav and his foundation exemplify the spirit of compassion, transformation, and inclusive growth via their work, which has a profound impact on individuals and communities around the world. His work exemplifies the power of acknowledging and nourishing the human spirit, creating a world in which everyone can reach their full potential and appreciate the beauty of life.

TESTIMONIALS

Journey of Soul - Karma - "We die in our twenties and are buried at eighty." Remember that nothing can stop someone who refuses to be stopped. "Most people do not fail; they simply give up." Shree Shambav deserves full credit. It allowed me to sit and consider what I might miss out on in life. The author has delved into every aspect of our daily lives. How can a seemingly insignificant change in these seemingly insignificant details bring us such joy? The Soul of Journey teaches you the "art of living" as well as the "art of dying."

Twenty + One Series - The rich cultural heritage offered a host in twenty + one short stories with incredible imagination, morals and values prevalent at a given time, influencing how people respond to a crisis or any situation. The author has recreated images with universal values and morals. The plentiful of fascinating from faraway lands would leave the modern play and story writers a cringe. The book supports trust and immeasurable values instilling hope for the new generations.

Death - "Shree Shambav's 'Death - Light of Life and the Shadow of Death' is an extraordinary masterpiece that delves deep into the profound questions surrounding our existence and mortality. The book's opening statement, 'Nothing ever truly dies; it simply ceases to exist in one form before resuming it in another,' sets the stage for a thought-provoking exploration of death's multifaceted nature. Shambav's remarkable ability to navigate the philosophical complexities of death and our universal fear of it is both enlightening and comforting. This book is a testament to the power of understanding and acceptance."

Whispers of Eternity - "Reading 'Whispers of Eternity' by Shree Shambav was a transformative experience that left me captivated from beginning to end. Each section of this exquisite collection delves into the myriad facets of existence, offering poignant reflections on life, death, and everything in between. Shree Shambav's verses are a testament to the beauty of language and the power of expression, inviting readers to embark on a journey of self-discovery and spiritual awakening. Whether celebrating life's simple joys or grappling with the complexities of human emotion, this book is a timeless companion that speaks to the heart and soul of every reader."

Life Changing Journey Series - "Life Changing Journey Series II Inspirational Quotes" is a remarkable collection that illuminates the path to self-discovery and personal growth. With its inspiring quotes and insightful reflections, this book serves as a beacon of light in a world often shrouded in darkness. Each quote offers wisdom, guidance, and encouragement, reminding readers of their inner strength and resilience. A must-read for anyone seeking inspiration and enlightenment.

Learn To Love Yourself - "A Heartfelt Guide to Authentic Self-Love." "Learn to Love Yourself" invites readers on a transformative journey to embrace their true essence in a world often focused on external validation. Through ten insightful chapters, it gently reveals principles of genuine self-love, guiding readers to deepen their connection with themselves. Beyond surface positivity, it encourages the cultivation of resilient self-acceptance, from embracing one's unique qualities to setting empowering boundaries. With inspiring stories and practical wisdom, this book is a trusted companion on the path to inner peace, fulfilment, and joy, helping readers build lives that reflect their authentic selves.

The Power of Letting Go - This book has been a gift to my spiritual journey. Shree Shambav's insights into attachment, personal growth cycles, and forgiveness are enlightening. The concept of seven-year cycles resonated with me, helping me understand the natural phases of life. I feel more empowered to let go of what no longer serves me and step into a life of freedom and fulfilment. A truly beautiful read!

A Journey of Lasting Peace - "A Journey of Lasting Peace" feels like a trusted friend guiding you through the maze of self-discovery. The 18 transformative principles are both practical and deeply resonant, addressing everything from gratitude practices to the art of letting go. Each chapter is infused with warmth and wisdom, making it easy to apply the concepts to my life. I particularly appreciated the emphasis on physical health's connection to mental well-being; it served as a wake-up call for me to prioritize my health. This book is an invaluable resource for anyone serious about personal growth!

Astrology Unveiled Series - "Profound, Logical, and Inspiring". What stands out in Astrology Unveiled is the author's dedication to making Vedic astrology logical and approachable. Each concept flows naturally into the next, backed by examples and exercises. The insights into karma and life cycles add a philosophical depth rarely seen in astrology books. Perfect for anyone seeking spiritual growth alongside astrological knowledge!

The Entitlement Trap - "Thought-Provoking and Challenging" The book challenges readers to confront their own sense of entitlement, and that's not easy—but it's essential. The Entitlement Trap doesn't offer a one-size-fits-all approach. Instead, it's a thoughtful, layered examination of how entitlement can limit our growth. The chapter on "Defining Your Own Hill" was particularly impactful, as it pushed me to reconsider which challenges are truly worth pursuing. A thought-provoking read for those willing to do the inner work to create a life they can be proud of.

Whispers of a Dying Soul - "A Soul-Stirring Reflection on Life's Unspoken Truths" - *Whispers of a Dying Soul: Unspoken Regrets and Unlived Dreams"* is a deeply moving exploration of the unexpressed emotions and unfulfilled aspirations that shape our lives in ways we often don't realize. This book invites readers to confront the powerful, often hidden impact of regret while guiding them through a journey of introspection and healing. Each page opens a space to reflect on the choices that define us—from moments of unspoken love to neglected passions—offering a gentle reminder to live authentically and courageously.

Whispers of the Soul - A Journey Through Haiku - is a mesmerising collection that speaks directly to the heart. Each haiku is a delicate brushstroke capturing life's fleeting beauty and timeless wisdom, inviting readers into moments of deep reflection and peace. This book is a balm for the soul, guiding us to find meaning in stillness and connection in simplicity. The themes of nature, love, and mindfulness echo universal truths, resonating with quiet, powerful grace.

It's a book to be savoured slowly, cherished deeply, and returned to often. Truly, a gift for anyone seeking calm and clarity in life's chaos.

Whispers of Silence - Unlocking Inner Power through Stillness by Shree Shambav is a rare gem that beckons readers to pause, reflect, and reconnect with their inner selves. In a world that never stops talking, this book offers a profound exploration of silence—not as a void but as a rich and transformative space.

From the first page, Shree Shambav's writing resonates deeply, blending scientific insights with spiritual wisdom in a way that feels both universal and deeply personal. The author's ability to bridge the tangible and the transcendent makes this book an invaluable guide for anyone navigating the chaos of modern life.

The Power of Words - Transforming Speech, Transforming Lives - "The Power of Words is a profound and enlightening guide that has transformed the way I approach communication. Shree Shambav masterfully uncovers the hidden influence of our words on relationships, self-perception, and overall well-being. This book doesn't just teach you how to speak; it inspires mindful communication that fosters connection and trust. The insights on replacing negative patterns like gossip and judgment with kindness and authenticity are truly life-changing. The practical strategies and engaging narratives make it an invaluable resource for personal and professional growth. A must-read for anyone striving to communicate with intention, clarity, and compassion. Highly recommended!"

The Art of Intentional Living: Minimalism for a Life of Purpose - "The Art of Intentional Living is a refreshing guide to finding clarity in a cluttered world. With practical wisdom and profound insights, it inspires you to simplify, prioritise, and live with purpose. A must-read for anyone seeking balance and fulfilment."

Awakening the Infinite: The Power of Consciousness in Transforming Life - "Awakening the Infinite is a transformative guide that expands the mind and nourishes the soul. With profound insights and practical wisdom, this book beautifully explores the power of consciousness, helping readers connect with their true purpose and inner potential. It is a journey of self-discovery, healing, and spiritual awakening, offering clarity and inspiration at every turn. A must-read for anyone looking to live with greater awareness, meaning, and authenticity."

ACKNOWLEDGEMENTS

To my grandfathers, grandmothers, mothers, fathers, aunts, uncles, neighbours, sisters, brothers, friends, and teachers, they poured in endless moral stories, retellings of Ramayana, Mahabharata, Puranas, Upanishads, and so on.

My teachers, neighbours, and kindred souls. Who provided us with a stage to perform wonderful Puranic stories and were gracious enough to acknowledge our efforts.

The artists and translators of epics have served as a source of inspiration, invigorating our spirits, making these works accessible, and enabling us to grasp the profound depths and deeper dimensions they contain.

I also cherish the stimulating conversations; I had with my wonderful mothers, Punitha Muniswamy and Uma Devi.

Our family's youngest member, Aadhya, who always overwhelmed me with questions, inspired this book.

I would likewise prefer to express gratitude to Mr Sivakumar, Mrs Roopa Sivakumar, Mr Akshaya

Rajesh, Ms Akshatha Rajesh, Ms Apeksha Prabhu, Mr Akanksh Prabhu, Mr Nikash Sarasambi, Mrs Spoorthi Nikash for their valuable inputs.

I must thank Mr Rajesh, Mr Savan Prabhu, Mrs Revathi Rajesh, Mrs Rajani Sarasambi, and Mrs Manju Reshma, who encouraged me and often suggested writing a book. Their unwavering belief that I had something valuable to offer kept me going during my writing sessions.

Love you all,

Shree Shambav

www.shambav.org

shreeshambav@gmail.com

BOOKS BY – AUTHOR

Journey of Soul - KARMA

"Journey of Soul – Karma" is a heartfelt exploration of life's profound truths in our increasingly complex world. Addressing challenges, inequalities, and the quest for meaning, this book brings the timeless concept of Karma into focus. It emphasizes Karma not merely as philosophy, but as a guiding principle for our daily lives, inspiring us to walk a path of integrity and purpose. Through this journey, readers gain insights into how actions shape destinies, encouraging a life aligned with truth and compassion. It's a beacon for those seeking a deeper, more fulfilled existence.

Death - Light of Life and the Shadow of Death

In *Light of Life and the Shadow of Death*, the enigma of mortality is approached with clarity and compassion. Death is an inevitable certainty, yet it casts a lingering shadow of fear over our lives, stirring grief and despair as we strive to prolong our time on earth. This profound work examines the fate of departed souls and the heavy emotions we attach to loss. Yet, it offers a path toward accepting death and finding peace amid life's uncertainties. Exploring our origins, ethical values, and purpose, it unveils the sustaining truth of existence. The shadow of death, though daunting, is reframed as a shared, universal experience—one that calls us to confront our deepest fears with wisdom and grace.

Whispers of Eternity 150 Plus - A Symphony of Soulful Verses

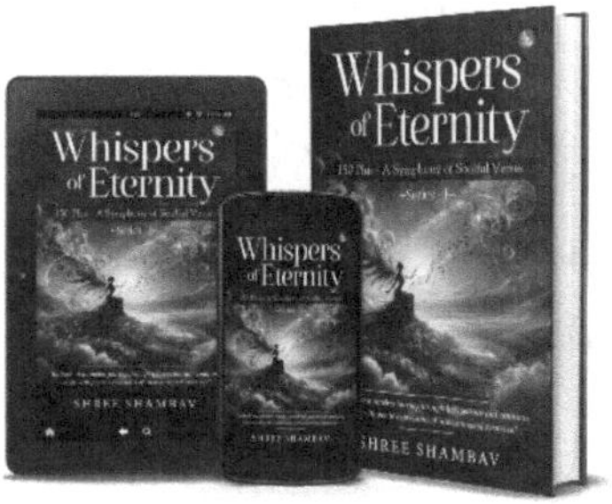

Step into the soul-stirring world of *Whispers of Eternity* by Shree Shambav, a collection of over 150 poems that capture the essence of the human experience. Divided into sections like "Through the Seasons," "Whispers of Hope," and "Threads of Unity," the book journeys through life's phases, emotions, and the universal connections that bind us all. Shree Shambav's verses touch upon nature, love, and spirituality, inspiring readers to find beauty in the everyday. Each poem is a finely crafted reflection, rich with insight and depth. *Whispers of Eternity* invites readers to pause, reflect, and embark on a timeless journey through the landscapes of the heart and soul.

Life Changing Journey Series I and II

In Life Changing Journey - 365 Inspirational Quotes Series I, Shree Shambav curates a powerful collection of 365 original quotes across fourteen chapters, each crafted to touch the heart of our daily lives. More than a simple compilation, this series speaks directly to personal experiences with wisdom and depth. Quotes like, "The most beautiful things are unseen but can be felt," echo the quiet beáuty of life's intangible moments. Another, "Giving up is easier; holding oneself up is wiser," provides a guiding light in challenging times. Life Changing Journey reveals the transformative power of carefully chosen words, inspiring readers to find strength and new perspectives on their paths. Through Shree Shambav's work, readers are reminded of the wisdom and resilience hidden within each day.

Twenty + One - 21 Short Stories Series I and II

In *Twenty + One - Short Stories*, Shree Shambav brings to life the often-overlooked characters of nature—trees, animals, and mountains—revealing their intrinsic worth beyond mere utility. With poetic personification, he gives voice to these silent beings, some of whom are lucky enough to have names, titles, and rare human protection. Mountains, usually seen as mere landmarks, are depicted with reverence, emphasising their enduring presence. The stories build a bridge between humans and the natural world, showing that pain, grief, and resilience are shared across all forms of life. Shambav invites readers to empathise with the silent struggles of trees and animals, inspiring a fresh perspective on ecology and our responsibility towards the environment. This collection is a call to honour our connection to nature, encouraging readers to foster compassion and respect for all life.

Learn To Love Yourself

Learn to Love Yourself is a powerful invitation to turn inward in a world focused on external validation and superficial measures. Through ten transformative chapters, each offering a key rule for self-love, readers are guided to uncover their inner beauty, cultivate personal strength, and develop a solid foundation of self-acceptance. This journey goes beyond momentary happiness; it's about building an authentic relationship with yourself that fosters resilience, joy, and fulfilment. From embracing your unique qualities and practising compassion to setting boundaries and pursuing what makes you come alive, this book provides essential insights and practical guidance. Let *Learn to Love Yourself* be your trusted companion on this path, inspiring you to unlock the limitless potential within and find true inner peace.

The Power of Letting Go

The Power of Letting Go invites you to release attachments, fears, and expectations, guiding you toward true inner freedom and joy. With deep insights, practical exercises, and timeless wisdom, this book equips you to face life's challenges with resilience and grace. It explores the essence of attachment, embraces the power of seven-year growth cycles, and teaches the art of forgiveness as a key to a fulfilled life. Each chapter brings concepts to life through relatable analogies and real stories, making profound ideas both accessible and engaging. Let this book serve as your beacon for self-discovery and spiritual awakening, helping you navigate uncertainties and unlock your potential for a joyful, meaningful existence.

A Journey of Lasting Peace

A Journey of Lasting Peace is a transformative guide to self-love, inner peace, and personal strength, where Shree Shambav leads readers through 18 powerful principles for discovering their true selves. Each chapter explores vital themes, from the quest for inner peace and the importance of self-awareness to the healing practices of mindfulness and yoga. Through practical strategies, reflective exercises, and heartfelt stories, this book offers a clear roadmap to a more authentic and fulfilling life.

Whether you seek to embrace imperfection, establish healthy boundaries, or reconnect with nature, A Journey of Lasting Peace provides the wisdom to navigate life's challenges and find enduring tranquillity. Perfect for anyone on a journey of self-discovery, this inspiring work gently reminds us that lasting peace starts within.

Astrology Unveiled: Series I and V

Astrology Unveiled: Foundations of Ancient Wisdom invites you to unlock the mysteries of astrology, offering timeless knowledge rooted in the teachings of ancient sages. This comprehensive guide explores fundamental principles like Rashi, Graha, Bhava, and Divisional charts, making it an essential resource for beginners and intermediate students alike.

With logical explanations and practical applications, Shree Shambav skilfully blends ancient insights with modern understanding. Rich in examples, detailed explanations, and engaging exercises, this book serves as an illuminating path to mastering Vedic astrology.

Embark on a transformative cosmic journey, discovering how astrology can unveil your destiny, guide life's choices, and support your spiritual growth.

The Entitlement Trap: Get Over It, Get On It

Are you feeling stuck in a cycle of blame and dissatisfaction? The Entitlement Trap: Get Over It, Get On It offers a transformative path to reclaiming your personal power. This insightful guide helps you break free from the mindset of victimhood and empowers you to take control of your life. Inside, you'll discover how to redefine success, prioritize your true values, and live with purpose. Through practical strategies, you'll learn to embrace simplicity, connect with nature, and leave a lasting legacy. Get ready to shift from powerless to empowered and create a life you love!

Whispers of a Dying Soul: Unspoken Regrets and Unlived Dreams

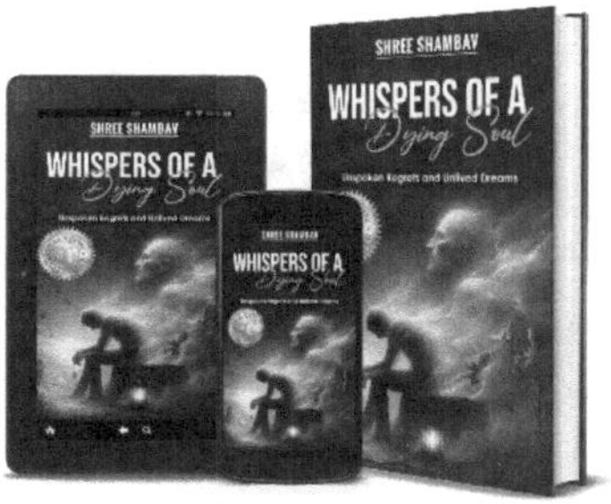

"Whispers of a Dying Soul", embarks on a profound journey that delves into the silent longings we often carry but seldom express. This powerful exploration uncovers the unspoken emotions that shape our lives—missed opportunities, unfulfilled dreams, and the quest for authenticity. Through heartfelt reflections and transformative insights, this book invites you to confront your regrets and turn them into powerful catalysts for growth and healing.

Whispers of the Soul: A Journey Through Haiku Series I to IV

"Whispers of the Soul: A Journey Through Haiku" is a poetic invitation to pause and rediscover life's hidden beauty. This transformative collection of haikus explores themes of nature, mindfulness, love, and the human journey, offering profound reflections on universal experiences. Divided into five series, the book delves into nature's elegance, the depths of inner stillness, the tenderness of human connection, the passage of life's seasons, and the mysteries beyond the self. Each haiku captures fleeting moments with timeless grace, guiding readers toward peace, self-discovery, and a renewed appreciation for life's simplest wonders. This is more than poetry—it's a soulful journey.

The Power of Words: Transforming Speech, Transforming Lives

The Power of Words: Transforming Speech, Transforming Lives illuminates the profound influence of our everyday language. This book explores how words can heal or harm, connect or divide, urging readers to embrace mindful communication. It delves into the "Sins of Speaking," such as gossip and judgment, while celebrating virtues like honesty, kindness, and authenticity. With practical strategies for transformation and a focus on the art of listening, Shree Shambav offers a roadmap to elevate our conversations. Perfect for both personal growth and professional development, this guide inspires readers to use their words to create peace, foster deeper connections, and lead a life of integrity and purpose.

The Art of Intentional Living: Minimalism for a Life of Purpose

In a world that celebrates more, The Art of Intentional Living invites you to embrace less. This powerful guide explores how minimalism can transform every aspect of your life—your space, your time, and your mind—by removing distractions and focusing on what truly matters.

Through simple yet profound principles, you'll learn to:

- Declutter your physical and digital space
- Prioritise what aligns with your values
- Create time for meaningful connections and experiences
- Cultivate a life of purpose, peace, and clarity

Awakening the Infinite: The Power of Consciousness in Transforming Life

In a fragmented world, Awakening the Infinite explores the power of consciousness to heal, transform, and unite. This book takes you on an experiential journey, revealing how awareness shapes reality and connects us to universal wisdom. Through spiritual teachings, introspection, and practical insights, it helps you uncover your soul's true purpose. With transformative practices, it guide you toward emotional healing, clarity, and personal growth. As you deepen your awareness, you'll forge a profound connection with yourself and the world around you. Embracing this journey leads to a life of mindfulness, authenticity, and purpose. Ultimately, it is an invitation to awaken the infinite potential within.

9 789334 251876

Printed at Repro India Ltd.